THE INSIDER SECRETS:
TO GET MONEY TO GROW YOUR BUSINESS

NATE KENNEDY
& MARK EVANS

Deal Maker Publishing, LLC
Mount Pleasant, South Carolina

The Insider Secrets of the World's Most Successful Financing Methods™

© Deal Maker Publishing, LLC

All Rights Reserved. This publication may not be reproduced, stored in a retrieval system, or transmitted in whole or in part, in any form or by any means, electronic, mechanical, photocopying, recording, or otherwise, except for personal use, without prior express written permission of the author.

ISBN #: 978-0-9788170-1-5

Printed in the United States of America

This publication is designed to provide competent and reliable information regarding the subject matters covered. However, it is sold with the understanding that the author and publisher are not engaged in rendering legal, financial, or other professional advice. If legal or other expert assistance is required, the services of a professional should be sought. The author and publisher specifically disclaim any liability that is incurred from the use or application of the contents of this book.

Please visit our website at www.MarkEvansDM.com

The author and publisher would like to acknowledge and thank the participants in this book who have granted us permission to cite their trademarked and copyrighted materials and publications.

ACKNOWLEDGEMENTS

This book is the result of the collaboration of many great people and for that we would like to extend our gratitude and appreciation to:

Our Families, for always believing in us and teaching us that we are able to achieve anything we want as long as we stay focused and set our goals high. Thank you so much for everything you have done for us.

Our Fiancés, Deena and Susan for being a tremendous support to us in life and our careers. You are amazing women and we are excited for the many great years that we have ahead of us. Who would have thought that one road trip would have created so many opportunities.

We would also like to extend our deepest appreciation and thanks to the people who participated in this book and made this dream a reality for us. Your kindness and support have helped us grow our careers to heights we never thought possible. You are all a driving force in this industry and we want to thank you for providing our readers with the opportunity to learn and become the best at what they do.

Last but not least, we would like to thank the reader. We hope you take this insider information and use it to achieve all your goals and dreams in life. Remember that goals are dreams, so as long as you live your dreams you will always reach your goals. You have the opportunity to do anything you want in life as long as long as you implement a path for your future. We wish you the best in everything you do.

We have been in the same position as most of our readers. We have spent time stressing where the next deal was coming from, if we were going to remain in this business, overworked and underpaid. It took us many years to eliminate all worries and enjoy our lives and careers. This is why we wanted to put all this powerful information into one book and give back to you.

Contents

Introduction		vii
One	Chris Hurn	7
Two	Jeff Desich	39
Three	Lee Arnold	73
Four	Sean Carpenter	119
Five	Melanie Ansel	155
Six	Darrell Hornbacher	189
Seven	Bob Norton	235
Websites You Need To Know About		281
About The Authors		283

Chapter One
Interview with Chris Hurn

Today we have a very special opportunity to learn from Chris Hurn, who is the CEO, President and co-founder of Mercantile Commercial Capital. He actively participates, in among other things, the business development, underwriting and marketing functions of the firm. Chris specializes in helping business owners buy their own office space, while increasing their cash flow. This unique niche has catapulted Mercantile Commercial Capital onto the Inc. 500, listed as one of the fastest growing companies in the nation. This quite frankly is an amazing accomplishment for anyone to reach and Chris has done it. So, this interview will give you some insight that you want to know so you can capitalize on working with Chris.

Chris, how are you doing today?

Doing great, Nate. How are you doing?

I'm doing fantastic. Today I want to talk about the specialized financing that you provide.

Okay.

And that being the 504 loan financing.

Internally, we don't call it the 504 anymore. We've rebranded it the SmartChoice Commercial Loan. And actually I think I said in some of the email correspondences that you and I were having about this call, it's a product that really should be so well-known it doesn't need to be in a book like this. It should be something that every mortgage professional out there offers their clients, that every business owner in America wants to partake in, and every investor in commercial real estate is looking to partake in when they can. We'll talk about some of the scenarios where that can happen in later. Unfortunately, it's still what I call the best-kept secret in commercial real estate financing.

Well let's start off real quick with that. Let's talk about how this can truly benefit the investor themselves.

The SmartChoice Commercial Loan is a program for owner-users. Now before anybody flips pages in the book, it can be used for investors as well. I'm going to give you some examples of how that works. The bottom line is that anybody who buys commercial property, whether it's a business owner or owner-user, or they're purely doing it for passive income, they're a true investor because they are looking at it as an investment tool. Commercial properties are one of the best assets out there to create wealth for anybody, whether it's another user or investor. The SmartChoice Loan is a tremendous tool to do it, and you're going to see why that is in just a second. I think it is the best commercial loan program out there for this particular purpose. In fact, I have one of these myself. I can't imagine there are many people reading these pages that are entrepreneurial enough, or believes in their product enough, to actually use it themselves. I don't know, maybe you've got a better group than I think, Nate. You probably do, knowing you. But people would probably agree with me that it's extremely rare to find a commercial banker that actually uses their own product. And we, in fact, do so.

The biggest reason why somebody wants to use this loan once they know about it, is it's really one of those rare products that sells itself once you're familiar with it. First of all, we do up to 90% loan-to-cost financing. So, that's a huge advantage versus going to an ordinary commercial bank, which, these days, is normally going to be 70 to 80% loan-to-value. And when I say loan-to-value it's really the lesser of the appraised value or purchase price. Very rarely. with the exception of perhaps hard money deals, can you get financing on whatever the embedded equity value of the property is. In other words, if you buy a property for $800,000 and it's appraised at a million dollars, very rarely are you going to be able to go to a traditional lender and get financing on the million. Most everybody's going to have you do the financing on the $800,000, and therein you've got embedded equity, as people like to say. So, that's a big difference between us and ordinary commercial banks.

We're actually looking at the total project cost. We're going to take the purchase price, any renovations you want to make to the property, and any soft costs related to the subject property. These could be impact fees, permitting fees, and/or architectural engineering fees, if you're going to do some renovations. We also include FF&E, which is furniture, fixtures, and equipment, and all closing costs. Put it all together and whatever that number is we'll usually finance up to 90% of it. So, there is the first reason why to use this program. You're actually putting down a third to half as much as what an ordinary commercial lender would want. Basically, it allows you to preserve more of your capital to do with it what you want. And for business owners, that's a huge advantage. Almost all business owners that I've encountered over the last 12 years of doing this, when given the choice of tapping all their accounts to come up with that 20, 25 or 30% down that the bank requires in order for them to buy that commercial property, or continue leasing their facility, are probably going to continue to lease. They have a fear that since capital is the lifeblood of most businesses, if they tap all their resources; they're not going to be able to weather the economic cycles as much as they would otherwise. With our situation they're able to put half to a third down and they're still able to preserve a lot of their capital to do what they want with it. Hopefully they'll use the equity savings to invest back in the business and actually grow the business even faster. So, that's one of the reasons, Nate.

The second reason is we actually do longer terms than ordinary commercial banks. We go out to 25 years as an amortization. From an interest rate perspective, we fix them for five or ten years. With an ordinary commercial bank these days they're so scared of their own shadows they're lucky if they're doing five or seven years fixed rates. And then they balloon it at the end of three, five, or seven. We generally do five and ten years rate resets, so it's fixed for five or ten years and then the resets at the end. I know in the residential world they probably call that an arm, but in the commercial world that's always called a fixed interest rate.

The third reason is probably the biggest one. The actual structure of these loans is such that almost half the loans, 44% to be exact, is the least expensive capital that is available to an owner of those small to midsize company out there in the market place. In fact, most of time, it's 100 to 150 basis points below market pricing. Meaning it's cheaper than what any bank would offer your client in America, and not only that, but it's fixed for 20 years which is virtually unheard of in the commercial real estate world. Most times people don't go out longer than 10 or 15 years. So, these are fixed at below market interest rates, and fixed for 20 years.

So, right there you have three big advantages, Nate that you don't normally see in a lot of ordinary commercial bank loans, conventional loans. And it just makes it a program that just sells itself when people know about it.

Oh, definitely. Within those three things, what is one of the smartest ways for someone to get involved in getting one of these loans? I know you run a pretty streamlined process.

I do. It's probably more streamlined than most commercial banks. There are unfortunately some misconceptions out there about loans that have government guarantees on them. You now have an agency of the government that may be guaranteeing the loan, in this case the Small Business Administration. There's a huge misperception that these loans take forever. And the reality is if you deal with a specialist like us, whether you're a mortgage professional, or investor, or another user; we've actually streamlined it so much that I would venture to say that we're faster than just about any other commercial bank out there. In fact, most of the time what happens is we hurry up and wait. We get everything done and then we tend to wait on third parties or on the borrower.

There's been plenty of times that we've had borrowers get to the closing table and they thank us because they would never have gotten to that point had we not driven the train. That happens all the time. And it's a little bit different in the commercial world then in the residential world. If the reader is used to the residential real estate mortgages there isn't a drive by for instance in the commercial world. For instance commercial appraisals can be 100 pages pretty easily. They're very comprehensive. They're a lot more expensive. You don't have $500 appraisals in the commercial real estate world. I'd say they start at about $2,000 and go up from there. Depending on the property type and the complexity of the project, I've seen appraisals cost up to $10,000 dollars. Now that's not the norm, most of them are in the $3,000 dollar range or so. You've got those commercial appraisers who are generally taking anywhere from three to six weeks to finish. You've got surveyors. If we can we'll get an updated survey, but sometimes you have to do a brand new survey. That could take up to a month.

With commercial property, you almost always get some variation of an environmental report. It could be as simple as a database search to see if there's any contamination nearby. What the ground ingredients are, if there's any oil plumes, if there's transformers, underground storage tanks or anything like that. The reason it's so important is because liability will transfer with commercial property. You don't want to get stuck with some big environmental problem that the previous owner basically pushed off to you. So, almost always on commercial real estate you're going to get environmental reports.

We try to keep it as simple as possible and keep the cost down as much as we can. If we don't need to get a phase one, we won't. If we don't need to get a phase two we certainly won't, but we've had numerous clients who've walked away from deals because it is contaminated. We go into phase two and do the slow boring tests and there's just nothing you can do about it. It's one of those that you just have to pass on, unless you want to incur that environmental liability. There's a lot of those types of things, third party type things that are happening simultaneously with our loans as they would with any commercial lender. Unfortunately we just have to wait until they're finished. It can be a little frustrating for borrowers. It's actually pretty frustrating to us, too. We don't get paid until the deal closes either. We just do everything we can. We push the process forward. We're fanatical about our follow-ups to make it happen and eventually it does happen. Any commercial real estate broker who's worth their pay at all is generally going to write real estate contracts for 60 to 90 days. There's some quick sales type situations, but again, you're really talking more like hard money situations where it's going to close in two or three weeks. But, most of the time it's just somebody looking to buy an office building, a warehouse, a restaurant. Generally speaking, it's going to be 60 to 90 days to close. Any competent lender that you work with ought to be able to close a loan within 45 days or less. We can certainly. So, does that answer your question Nate?

Yes, it does. There's a lot that goes into getting a commercial loan done, and the key is having a strong team to do it. I know you guys have grown at a pretty good pace, and I think you have a pretty unique way of bringing people on to make sure that they're the most efficient as possible when they join your team.

Absolutely. It's funny; I've had numerous people, reporters, authors, talk to us in the past about this. We have a very unique entrepreneurial corporate culture, which makes us stand out very differently from just about every other commercial banker out there. We also have a very young company, and by young, I just don't mean the length that we've been in business. Although, that's relatively young as well, we've been in business about six years. But I mean the actual ages of the people working here. It would shock people to know that they were dealing with somebody more than likely in their 20's. When you take away myself and three other employees who are all over the age of 35, what you're left with is an average age of about 26. That would probably strike fear in the hearts of most bankers, but it was very purposely done by me.

For virtually everybody that's here, this is the first corporate job they've ever had. There's about a half dozen of them that were previously interns or apprentices, as I would like to think of it, that I hired full time. They don't come here with baggage. There's way too many people in the banking and the financial services world that will hop from one bank to another and take their baggage with them. I didn't want that. I formed the company in my mold, so I train my employees my way. They hustle, they're energetic, they're like sponges because they soak up all the information out there. They really bust their butts and that's what you want in a lender. You want somebody who's looking at ways to try and get a deal done, as opposed to figuring out ways to put stops to it.

And that is really, really evident as you know, Nate. In an economy like what we're in right now with the banking and the lending crisis that's going on. We're having what's shaping out to me one of our best year ever. And when I tell that to people they scratch their head and think I've got three or four eyeballs, and they don't understand how that's possible. It's possible because we're very focused on what we do. We believe we're the best at what we do nationwide and we can be because our focus allows us to be more creative, to spend more time on a deal when needed and to drive that deal home to closing when it needs to close by a specific deadline. We just have a lot of advantages that our banking brethren don't have. It's a major differentiator for us, and it works very well. And I would expect it to continue. It certainly helps when a lot of our competition falls by the wayside. You know the strongest survive in the economic market place, much like in life.

And that's the thing too. Where residential is in complete disarray right now, the commercial division is definitely growing.

Well, to some extent it is. I would've probably agreed with you three or four months ago but I would say right now, we're doing this in September of 2008, that commercial is starting to suffer a little bit. It's mostly because of the problems from the residential side that is seeping into the risk aversion that most banks have when doing any new deals, be it commercial or residential. On the commercial side, it's impacting their ability to take on additional risk. A lot of banks don't have the liquidity to take on additional risks. They have been hit by the regulators, so they've tightened down. It's unfortunate because that's going to translate into a kind of a self-filling prophecy. If you say that we're in an economic recession long enough, then pretty soon the bankers say, "Well maybe we're in an economic recession and therefore we don't want to do anymore deals." The moment that they stop doing deals then pretty soon we're in an economic recession. Some of that's happening and it's unfortunate.

But as I tell people all the time, now is perhaps a once in a generation period to buy discounted assets, in particular commercial real estate. I have seen prices just plummet. I'll give you an example of an office condo pretty nearby to here that the pricing has literally plummeted by 50%. Maybe it was priced a little bit high to begin with but to come down 50% is awfully significant. It amazes me. It was probably roughly worth what they were selling if for per square-foot basis, but when you lop off half of that, it's a steal of a lifetime. Courageous business owners and courageous investors are out there right now buying up discounted commercial property. And when everything turns around, because it always does -- everything goes in cycles -- they're going to be sitting pretty having minted a fortune.

Yeah and it's right now there's a lot of investors buying a lot of property everywhere. It's a great time. Let's get into some of the nitty gritty. Let's go over a couple of deals that you guys have done recently, some real life analysis of deals.

Let me give you some examples. I should probably tell you that the property types we finance are free standing, with the exception of commercial condos. But free standing offices, industrial space like warehouses, restaurants, limited service hotels, daycare centers, assisted living facilities, veterinarian offices, medical offices, funeral homes, and car washes to list some. It's a pretty broad spectrum, as you can see.

Lately, we've done an inordinate amount of limited service hotels this year. They've been mostly flagged hotels, like Days Inn, Sleep Inn, Holiday Inn Express, Hampton Inn.

We do a lot of daycares…and let me back up here a second, Nate. The commonality of everything that we do is to create wealth for our borrowers. It's one of the simplest ways for a business owner to create wealth. We like to think of it as the three American dreams that Fannie Mae and Freddie Mac have beat into our heads for years.

The first American dream is to own your own house. Well, for anybody who's in business for themselves the next American dream, of course, is to be their own boss, And then the logical next step from that is to actually own their own commercial real estate property, for the same exact reason that they moved out of their apartment into a house one day years ago. It is the same rationale for why business owners ought to move out of their leased facility to own commercial property. A lot of folks just get tunnel vision and focus on putting out fires, seeing patients, making widgets, etc. and forget that there's this really simple wealth creation strategy of converting that rental payment into a mortgage payment that actually builds equity and appreciable assets. And so, the extra strategy for a lot of business owners is that they plan to one day sell their business or shut their business down. Maybe they want to gift their business to their kids, but let's be honest, it's probably not going to go public someday, a very, very small percentage of businesses ever go public. Most of them are bought or shut down.

And so if that's your extra strategy -- and I'm just being honest with everyone – then the sooner you can extract more wealth from your business the better off you'll be. One of the simplest things to do is after you've established yourself in the marketplace which usually that takes anywhere from three to five years, and you will have hopefully built up some capital. If you use the SmartChoice Commercial Loan, without putting a lot of capital down, but you can immediately convert that rental payment into a mortgage payment. What I try to do for probably 90% of my borrowers is separate out the real estate asset from the operating company. And so you'll have an operating company, maybe it's some sort of an LLC, over here on the left and on the right you've got this real estate holding company, otherwise known as an eligible passive concern which is an LLC to do nothing but own that real estate. We tie it together with what's called a master's lease. It's a 100% master's lease between the operating company and the holding company.

Then some day in the distant future when you sell your business, you sell the operating company, but you retain the real estate asset. And then whoever buys the operating company may become a tenant, or you just turn around and sell the property as well and take your chips off the table. But the bottom line is that you have flexibility. You have options at that point if you take on this strategy. If you want to continue to throw your money away from now until eternity renting your facility, that's certainly your choice. I just don't think that makes a heck of a lot of sense from the perspective of trying to increase your net worth, which is what every business owner ought to be contemplating. So, I just wanted to throw that out there, Nate. I think it's pretty important.

It's very important.

Yes. Some of the deals we've done lately…I'm just looking at a closing loan list. We've done a manufacturing company in Missouri, a daycare in Louisiana, a non-franchise restaurant in Texas, a carpet cleaning company in Florida, a pool service company in Georgia, a pharmacy in New Jersey, an auto repair shop in Florida, a youth hostel in Pennsylvania, a lighting company in Colorado, a martial arts academy in Illinois, a lawn maintenance company in Indiana. Oh this is one of my favorites, a satellite television and cell phone company combined, in Alaska of all places. A cosmetic surgeon in Florida, two Laundromats in Indiana, a daycare in Virginia, an accounting firm in Florida, a law firm in Florida, a limited service hotel in Louisiana, you want me to keep going?

I'll tell you what, that's quite a bit. You guys definitely handle a lot of different properties, which is amazing. And I think that it's good for our readers to understand and know the type of realm that you guys can do.

Yes exactly. I mean I could go on. There's a lot of interesting stuff in here. There's a bread company…that's kind of one of my favorites.

Well, how would you go about doing, say, the bread company? You said they're one of your favorites. What is the fastest way a business owner could go about purchasing their own property?

Well, there's actually an interesting story behind this one. It's called the Old Hearth Bread Company and they had heard about us from a commercial real estate broker, which is one of our biggest referral sources, by the way. For the mortgage professionals reading this, you can't just go walk into a commercial real estate brokerage firm and expect them to turn over deals to you. You have got to show some confidence. You have to know what you're doing, and it's going to take a lot of time before you develop the relationship where they just willingly turn over their deals to you to finance. So, Old Hearth was referred to us by a commercial real estate broker here in town and they had heard about us. Their bank did exactly what I said earlier, Nate, which was that they offered to do the deal at 80% loan-to-value. It was a ground up construction project, which is really where we stand out so much more than an ordinary bank. Again, getting back to what I said earlier about loan-to-value, a lot of times for ground up construction projects, bankers will require the borrowers to put 20 to 25% down. And then they've got to pay all those closing costs and soft costs out of pocket.

So, when all is said and done they may put 30 to 35% into this whole project. Whereas in our situation they still only have 10% down on the total project cost. So, that made a dramatic difference to these guys. These guys sell a lot of their baked goods, like pastries and breads to the big hospitality industry here in Orlando. Think of them as a wholesaler. You're not going to go to a grocery store and pick up their bread or pastries, but if you stay at a hotel in Orlando there's a very strong likelihood that you're eating some of their product. Also, they wanted somebody to deal with who understood them, who "got" them. We've often been called the "entrepreneurial bankers". We tend to operate in a much more entrepreneurial fashion than most of these conservative bankers in our industry.

So, we immediately resonated with them. They realized that we were very much like them in that we wanted to figure out a way to get their deal done, and that we thought it was important for them to put down as little capital as possible. See, what a lot of people don't understand, bankers included, is there is what I call a continuum of risk, with the business owners at one end of the spectrum and the commercial bankers at the other end. When you lower the risk to the banker by putting more capital down, you automatically and fundamentally increase the risk to the business owner, and vice versa. What's interesting is because our product happens to be one that has a government guarantee in place, there's not nearly as much risk as people would think there is to the banker. And therefore, we can offer a loan product that is much more favorable to the borrower and will allow them to be confident, courageous and comfortable enough to use their equity savings to actually redeploy into their business and grow their business that much faster. That's how what we do fundamentally is basically like an economic development program, in many respects. And one of the things that we measure regularly is how many jobs we create.

We're closing in on 3,000 jobs that we've helped create in the last six years by doing the financing that we do and that's a whole other discussion we can get into, but Old Hearth needed the deal done fast. They needed to deal with competent people to do the ground up construction project. They wanted to put as little money down, and we just meshed with them well on all these points. It didn't take very long for them to know that we obviously knew exactly what we were doing, that we actually had more specialized knowledge than the other lenders. They stroked us a check, we went to issue a commitment letter and we started working towards closing and it was as simple as that. Now there were some delays again with the contractor in terms of getting a final construction contract done, and some of the plans and specs we had to go back a couple of times in dealing with the municipality or what not. But in general, from a financing perspective it was about as easy and straightforward of a process as they could ever have imagined. And that's really what they needed. They needed somebody they could trust to just take this project off their hands and run with it, and that's exactly what we did.

And that's what a lot of businesses want. They want a lender or mortgage professional who can find them the best overall deal, and by the way, that does not always necessarily mean the lowest common denominator, otherwise known as price. I said the best overall deal which is a combination of different variables, price being one of many. Monthly payment terms, collateral, down payment, all sorts of other variables that factor into that decision. They want somebody to basically just take the whole process off their hands, so we actually created what's called the Commercial Loan Concierge™ Program. I don't believe these guys availed themselves of it, but we've had plenty of borrowers do that. Physicians for example, whose time is more valuable, spend in their business. They go and do Commercial Loan Concierge™ Program where we have them fill out an authorization form to let us deal with their accountants, their real estate broker, their attorney, their office manager, in order for us to go get all the documents we need so that they're pretty much hands-free. And we let them know when to sign some documents, which probably take five or ten minutes in the middle of the process. Then we call them and say, "Which of the following three days would you like to close this loan on?" And they show up for the closing table and that's pretty much it.

It's about as hands-off of a process as you can ever imagine and people love that. They just think that's the greatest thing ever, because there is this perception that buying commercial property is going to be such a nightmare process. That their regular business is going to have to grind to a halt while they take care of all these things. At least with us, and I can only speak for our perspective, it doesn't have to be that way at all for our borrowers. So, it's a real good experience for everybody, and that's what we really try to provide every single time. We want it to be the best lending experience possible to our borrowers. And a lot of other people that we compete against aren't even thinking in terms of experience. Frankly, they're not even thinking many times at addressing the immediate need. That's why bankers sometimes have the poor reputation that they do, the stereotype that exists about bankers. We try to stay above the fray and just do right by our borrowers and help them create wealth for themselves as easily and efficiently as possible. That's why we have 90% of our business coming to us through referrals.

The concierge service that you do is unbelievable. That's huge for anyone in this market because like you said, the business owners and the people that you work with, they make their money by focusing on their business. So, letting them do just that by taking control of the process and handling it for them is huge. That they would trust you to take care of it this way, that's your reputation preceding you.

Sometimes when I talk to mortgage professionals they're shocked when I tell them we've close loans in 32 states around the nation. We've only met the borrowers in maybe two or three of those states. Everybody else, we've never even met them. You could only do that when you have enough competence on the phone, fax and email because in fact they do trust us and we do what we say we're going to do, which in this day and age is a rare thing. I hate to say it, but it really is. My view has always been that we actually know how to read third party reports unlike a lot of people we compete against. So it's not really necessary for us to go out to visit the property. I've got a hundred-page commercial appraisal. I know what the property's worth. I know what it looks like. If I need to, I'll pull it up on Goggle Earth and look at it, but there it is. I know what the environmental situation is like from their reports. I have the survey. I've got the title. I've got all the information I need to know to make a decision in addition to the financials of the borrower. But that's not something that probably could have happened 10, 15, or even 20 years ago, because the world just moved on.

I think what separates us a lot of times from ordinary commercial bankers is that they still want the borrower to do the dog and pony show every two or three weeks leading up to the closing of their loan. We don't make our borrowers do that. We know that the biggest asset they have is time, and that's why we try to take as much off their plate as possible, and to make it happen. And you know what, we've got raving fans from our clients. If you go on our web site you'll find literally hundreds of testimonials from borrowers and their advisors that have dealt with us in the past. We've now closed loans from Alaska to Puerto Rico, New York to California and everywhere in between. So, we must be doing something right. Which is not what anybody else does in our industry.

Well, that's probably why it's right, huh?

Yes that's what I think, but you know this is heresy in my industry.

You mentioned a little bit earlier about how business owners can accomplish wealth creation by owning commercial property. How important is that especially today with the way that the stock market, bonds, CD's, and residential real estate is performing?

Well, I don't need to tell you or the listeners or the readers that the stock market constantly on a rollercoaster ride. This week it happens to be down. Although, now it's up from where it was this morning and the yields on bonds are plummeting. Which by the way is a good thing for borrowers of capital, especially in long-term commercial real estate financing, because almost everything is tied in some way to the ten year treasury yield which has been plummeting lately. Pretty much coinciding with Freddie Mac and Fanny Mae being taken over, this is exactly what I predicted. CD rates are sucking wind right now. Residential real estate is problematic at best. Clearly there are values out there to be had. It's a function of do you dip your toe in the water that has a lot of piranha in it, or not? That's a question you'd have to answer. But then what does that leave? I guess you could go buy gold if you want. Although, gold's even come down from their highs in the last month or two, along with oil and a lot of other commodities have been dropping.

Commercial real estate has kind of held up pretty well, with the exception of my egregious example earlier about the 50% discount. Commercial real estate actually held its ground pretty well. And I don't think a lot of people think about buying their commercial real estate as a way to round out their investments and to diversify their investment portfolio and I think that needs to change, because as I said it's one of the easiest assets that you can borrow against. It is effectively what you're doing when you finance it to help grow wealth, and to use the leverage to your advantage. I think now is a great time to be doing it, because every other asset class that you could take a look at is sub-par at best.

Definitely and you know I'm going to bring it back. You have created something that is actually amazing, but how did you really get your start and decide to do this? It's kind of opening up the book a little bit here and just getting that idea where it came from.

I'll give you the abbreviated version. When I got out of grad school, I worked for a high tech start-up before it became really fashionable. I was in sales and marketing for a couple of years. Actually, even before that I have to confess, it's a little bit embarrassing and I don't tell a lot of people this, but there was a recession when I got out of grad school and it was really tough to find a job. After refusing some $18,000 to $20,000 a year jobs, because I thought, "How the hell am I going to live on that?" I finally swallowed my pride and after about three or four months of real heavy job searching and God knows how many résumés, cover letters, and interviews I went on, I took a temp job. It turned out that I was so good at what I did that as soon as they could do an early buy-out of the temp contract, they exercised it and hired me full time. I was in sales and marketing. So, I made a little bit more money than what I expected by that point.

I continued to invest in my education though, and that's a really important thing. I was out of traditional schooling but I'm one of these guys who's always learning, who's always investing in my ongoing education and so I'm constantly devouring things. I'm a voracious reader. I put off a lot of a lot of immediate gratification that I could otherwise have had, which I saw a lot of my colleagues doing, so that

I could actually redeploy my capital into new investments whether, they be real investments or investments in myself that would hopefully pay off later on. So, I did that for a couple of years.

Then a headhunter came around who worked for GE Capital, and they made me an offer I couldn't refuse. So, I left the high tech start-up. I think I was employee number 80 or 82 and by the time I left, they were over 800 so that shows you how fast that company grew. I joined GE and worked for them for about six months in the Washington DC area. Then they offered me a choice to move to either Charlotte, Denver or Orlando. I'm originally from downstate Illinois outside of Peoria and as any enlightened Midwestern boy will tell you the holy land is where the sun's at. And so I said, send me to Orlando. I had to convince my wife that that was the right thing to do, because she kind of wanted to go to Denver. She'd grown up skiing, where I never had anything strapped to my feet other than shoes. I wasn't too keen on going to Charlotte, it was kind of a sleepy town; it's obviously done a lot better over the years.

So I was really happy in Orlando and we put some roots down. I worked for GE Capital for a while. Eventually Heller Financial made me an offer I couldn't refuse to run the local shop for them. Then about a year and a half later GE turns around and buys Heller, which I often have said they didn't need to spend billions of dollars to get me back, they probably could have just doubled my salary. But I came back and then I left again.

And at this point, I had decided to become a management consultant and I had a good time doing it. I traveled around the country, probably way too much. I made some serious impact in the lives of the businesses that I worked with, and was mostly doing financial strategic operational organizational consulting. But I quickly became the go-to-guy for the strategy and marketing aspects of all the engagements. And so, that's really where my expertise lies.

Eventually, my wife and I we had our first child a daughter, and I just decided I had to knock this off. I've got to get off the road a little bit. During all this time by the way, I continued to invest in myself, commercial real estate and a bunch of different things. One of the guys I had met through the commercial real estate development that I had done was running the second largest commercial real estate brokerage firm here in Orlando. A united affiliated firm and he had just lost his CFO. I had known him for a while and he knew I was a consultant. He kind of lamented to me, and I said, "Well here's what you really need in a consultant". Remember I was a consultant so I was telling him exactly what he needed in a CFO. And he said, "Why don't you just do it?" and I said, "Well, okay," and I came back and got into it.

About the same time I said, "You know I have this idea for a commercial lending company," and he said, "Okay." He'd actually run four different banks as their president/CEO. The last bank he had sold a couple of years before and had made a lot of money doing it. I think he really wanted to get back into banking and what I brought him was kind of a vehicle for which to do it. Which was our company, but here's the catch. I basically came to him and said, "Look I want to start my own lending company. I want to pretty much focus on one primary lending product." Which when we told people this who we've known over the years, they thought we were crazy because bankers just don't do that. You don't do one product. You try to be all things to all people. You know you want to have 40, 50, 60 different products and services to offer your clients but I wanted to do one, because I wanted to be the best at one. And then I said, "Well then here's the kicker. The one also happens to have a government guarantee. So, it's kind of a government sponsored lending product." Which usually that was the point that people would walk away laughing at us, saying that we're going to fail miserably, and then why would we even bother with that type of thing.

So, that was almost six years ago. And obviously, we've proved the skeptics wrong. We've grown tremendously. We've now financed somewhere north of 330 million dollars in total projects all around the country. Most of that has an average project size of a million to five million dollars, something like that. These are not huge projects, but it's like I say, its one business owner at a time. We created our image. The corporate culture definitely represents us, and we've had a ton of fun doing it.

So, that's my background and in the middle of all that, I became a business coach which allowed me to do, "group consulting", as I call it. It's basically consulting without the travel and more than one client in the room.

Recently, being a practitioner of what I preach, I went out and bought a discounted asset, which was another business -- a franchise. We are now the new franchisors of a very successful upscale barbershop club, which is actually little known outside of Orlando, that we're going to be franchising all around the country soon. One of the things that make it unique is that they've done no marketing historically; it's all been word of mouth. I suggested a few minutes ago that I'm kind of a marketing guy and I think I know how to do it really well. So, I'm going to be adding some marketing expertise to dramatically help this company. We're going to tweak it a little bit and other than that, it's pretty good to go. I think this is a phenomenal concept.

It has not been lost on me that in the last major economic crisis, recession or whatever, right after Jimmy Carter was elected the franchising industry actually boomed. It booms during these cycles mostly because people are laid off from big corporate jobs and they looking to go do something else. They don't necessarily want to start something from scratch; they don't want to have to reinvent the wheel. They'd rather take a turnkey system and grow it from there. They want to buy something they can earn a good living with and have some fun. That's kind what our barber clubs are. You didn't even know that last one.

I didn't even know that. I'm thinking of waiting for that franchise to get started here.

You're particularly going to love the name, because it's Kennedy's All-American Barber Club™.

All right.

You like that?

Yeah I do. I do. And it's like you mentioned, you know some of your marketing worked with you in the past and it's unbelievable what you guys are able to do. You touched on this earlier; I don't think that people educate themselves enough.

No, they don't.

I really wish and hope people take that from this as well. Letting them know education is huge and that the reason you are so successful and your business grows the way it does is because of the education that you constantly bring yourself and investing in yourself.

Now, if someone wanted to move forward and get involved in getting a loan done or look at your franchise coming up here, what's the best way for them to reach you?

The best way is to go to **www.TheSmartChoiceLoan.com**. They can also email me at **info@mercantilecc.com**. That's for my company, Mercantile Commercial Capital.

If they're seriously interested in the franchise, they can go to **www.kennedysbarberclub.com**. And they can get a hold of me there.

The other thing I would tell you, and we really didn't get into it today, the lending program that we specialize in is for owner-users. Investors can sort of pool their resources with an owner-user. And it makes a tremendous way to buy commercial property. In other words Nate, if you had some capital and wanted to buy an office building down the street, and you have a buddy who's an architect, and his business can cover the debt service, and you're the one who's providing some of the capital; we would look at you as a combined entity and that's another way to do one of these deals. A lot of people don't realize that, but you don't even have to be an investor. It could be an architectural firm combining with an adult daycare firm, for instance on the same property. We could do it that way. You know the key there obviously is you've got to structure your legal documents correctly, especially with partner buyouts. You're going to be partnering with somebody who maybe you don't know real well, and that can sometimes pose problems for people, but it's better to put it all in writing because memories tend to fade over time. So, those are some of the things that you can do and that make our program a little more unusual. It sort of expands it from just being an owner-user program to actually giving some other opportunities to investors. I just wanted to make sure I pointed that out.

Yes, definitely. I think that's very important. Okay are there any parting words that you'd like to get out to our readers?

I just think it's important to deal with people that know what they're talking about, and practice what they preach. When you buy commercial property, it's important to try to work with the smartest people there. People that understand that it's all about cash and cash return, which is clearly one of the things we talk about all of the time. You want to deal with competent people. People that can hustle on your behalf, and everything I just said there is completely 180 degrees opposite of what most folks in the mortgage professional world are probably used to dealing with in bankers. But again, back to what you said in the beginning, there's a reason for the success we've had. There's a reason we've grown as fast as we have, versus a lot of people in our industry that are actually going out of business right now. There's been a definite weeding out of the least strong in the mortgage market place.

It's exciting to interview someone who's done some great things, and I'm excited for our readers to be able to read this, and absorb it and move their life forward, especially to be able to use you, and your expertise to help grow their business.

I appreciate it as always, Nate. Anything I can do to help you out or your readers or listeners, I'll be happy to give it a try.

All right thanks so much Chris.

Chapter Two
Interview with Jeff Desich

Hey Jeff, Mark Evans

Hey Mark how are you?

Good! Thanks.

Okay. Let's get started. Let's first start off by asking, what is Equity Trust Company?

Sure again with Equity trust, we are a custodian of self directed IRAs, and that is kind of the formal way you could kind of explain it, but I like to say that what we do at Equity Trust Company is we help investors make tax-free profits. We show investors who have a level of knowledge and expertise or a desire to invest in certain investments, and most of the time it is real estate, but what we do is we show investors how to structure their deals so that we can reduce or eliminate if possible the taxes that would occur in their normal business dealings if they didn't have the IRAs or the ROTH IRAs. So really what we do is we help people learn how to do similar deals that they are doing every single day, and how to do it in a tax-free or tax-deferred environment. That is obviously through the retirement accounts or through the IRAs.

Okay great. Could you explain just a little bit more in detail kind of what an IRA is. I mean I understand tax deferred and all that, but can't people pull from a 401K and transfer it into a self-directed?

Definitely. Well to start off with an IRA is basically an account that the government has given us that allows us to accumulate or grow wealth without the hindrance of tax.

Go Grab Your $247 of FREE Gifts at www.InsiderSecretsMoney.com

Basically with this account every year we are able to make a contribution or to put money into the account, and those contribution limits vary depending on the type of IRA and how old you are, but for most Americans with a traditional or a ROTH which is the most common, they are going to be able to contribute either five or six thousand dollars. Each year we are able to put money in through a contribution, once the money is there inside of the account then you go forward and start to make investments with those contributions and obviously all of the returns on those investments are going to accumulate again without the hindrance of tax. Then once the individual is ready to start taking money out they are going to take distributions. So we have contributions when you put money in, and you have the distribution when you take the money out. As long as you take the money out after 59-1/2 then you are not going to have any penalties, but if you do need to get at the money before 59-1/2, unless it is for a hardship, there is a 10% penalty. So once you reach 59-1/2 you then have access to that money, and we can talk about the ROTH and traditional in just a minute and maybe the differences between the two, but then obviously once you reach that 59-1/2 you can start to pull the money out.

As you had asked the question, there are really three ways to get money into an IRA. The first one we talked about was the contributions and that is each year, again putting money in from your own pocket. The second way is through a transfer an IRA transfer, if you have an existing

IRA anywhere else, a bank, a brokerage firm, an insurance company, those can all be transferred to Equity Trust Company when then you will have access to those funds to invest in what you want to. The third way is through a rollover from a 401K or a 403B, many people obviously are switching jobs these days. I read a figure not long ago that they said 7 or 8 times in a career is kind of the average these days, so every time you leave a company, either you are downsized or you quit, or you were fired, you retire, or for whatever reason, if you leave that company you are able to roll that 401K over to an IRA and obviously that is the third way that you can get money into your equity trust IRA, and then obviously you have the freedom to start to invest in what you know and what you understand.

There you go absolutely. Okay great. We have with what is going on in the markets and all this stuff that we have going out there Jeff, what do you think? I mean I am not a huge fan of the stock markets anyway because I don't understand it and I don't like to put my money in those kinds of things. How can you give me an example of a real estate transaction from start to finish from an IRA and explain the benefits and the downfalls of utilizing a service like this?

Sure. What I will do to is just in the example is just kind of give some round numbers to make the point. Obviously, these are based off of kind of real life deals; the example I am going to give is based off of real life deals that we see every single day here within the company, but just to make the number a little bit easier to follow. You had mentioned

Go Grab Your $247 of FREE Gifts at www.InsiderSecretsMoney.com

about the market and what we are going through right now and really over the last 10 years or so we have seen two distinct trends really take form. The first one is obviously Americans desire or realization that their broker isn't the end all in terms of securing their financial future. In that many Americans have decided that they want to take a more active role and recognize that I just can't open an account somewhere and meet with an advisor once and then 20 years from now hope that I am going to have enough money to live on for the rest of my life, or that will provide me the lifestyle that I want to have. Even just stopping in to see that person once a year isn't necessarily enough and rather than wait to that point where it is almost too late to realize that has occurred and many Americans are taking the direction of taking control. So, we see that as one major trend and the other one is the real openness to alternative investments.

I think your comment was right on with many Americans today and if they didn't feel it after the tech bubble, they are definitely feeling it now, and that is Wall Street...there has to be something more than just Wall Street, the stocks and the mutual funds and people making decisions that are great for them, but not necessarily for me, the shareholder or me the retirement holder, and so realizing that there are a lot of great investment opportunities out there and more specifically even close to home, in your own city or region. There is obviously economic growth going on everywhere and it is a lot easier to make it 10, 20, 30% return on a million dollar investment than it is on a $10 billion dollar investment so there is a lot more smaller deals that are out there and obviously that opens up a lot of potential.

Absolutely and if I hear you right, what you are really saying is the consumer is becoming more educated because they are taking more responsibilities for their financial future, right?

You got it and that is exactly it, that and then again that there is more choices for them now or at least they are aware of more choices.

Exactly, but unfortunately like you said most people never realize it until they get hit 50% of their nest egg is taken from them through a bad investment etc. right and then they are like, "Wait I better figure this out."

Exactly. It is that and then you just lost half of your money and you want an explanation, just tell me why, what happened. Well the market goes one way or the other or well if I had just lost half of my money, I want somebody to explain why it happened, and I don't think many, well I shouldn't go that far, but I think that many advisors would have difficulty in trying to explain why the things happened on Wall Street that did.

Yeah and at that point if they knew why they wouldn't have lost your money, right?

Exactly.

So it is really all about preparing correctly through education. I know you guys offer education and that is

what this whole purpose of this book and CD and audio is, is to really educate you and like you said, know that there are other options available to you if you are serious about wanting to do more with your money.

Definitely. When it comes down to like we were talking about with a real estate transaction, for the majority of our clients what the IRA really allows them to do is again take control and use their own knowledge and expertise. There are thousands of our clients that can walk into a house and can look at a house within 5 minutes and size up what needs to be done to the house, what its rental potential might be, what its market value might be, and to ask them to do that on Morgan Stanly Stock or GE or IBM or any other company for that matter, unless you are following the market or you are some analyst who hands all this information to you, it is difficult. With real estate though this is a great vehicle for again thousands or tens of thousands of Americans that understand real estate and that they can really take an active role to find great deals to invest in with their IRA. We see great returns from our customers just great success stories and they just keep coming and coming and coming because people are able to understand what they are buying and take advantage of the market. It is from Boston Massachusetts to Los Angeles, Hawaii to Florida, all across the country clients are taking advantage of this. We have clients in all 50 states and the types of real estate people are buying it across the board. It could be from raw land to a mobile home to a tax lien, to a single family home, to commercial real estate, a lot of great opportunities out there for people to take advantage of and again it allows them to invest to our clients to invest in what they know and what they understand.

Absolutely and because you can see it, touch it, feel it, smell it, you can do all the great things with a hard asset, and I think there is nothing more valuable than that. Especially with today's market the way the prices are in real estate, they have been beat up as well, but if you can get a discount on today's prices, you are way ahead of the curve.

Exactly. That is where again I would say that the majority of our clients, what they are able to do is really make money when they buy in real estate, not when they sell. I think it is a huge distinction recognizing that when they are purchasing the property, like you said if they can buy it at a discount off of today's value. So let's say the house is worth $100 a year ago and today it is worth $70 and if I can buy it for $50, okay I have already made my money or assume that I can…if the market is at 70 I already have some built in profit there. It is kind of investing versus come more the speculating where I am going to buy the property today for a 100 and hope that in 5 years it is going to be worth 120, well if the market is at 70 you are hoping when you sell here, not when you buy.

Let me give you a typical example again even just using rounded numbers, but you know again this varies from region to region in terms of prices, if you are in California you can add an extra zero on there, but just say $100,000 property right now in a neighborhood and our clients again on a typical rehab property, they will come in and they will find a motivated seller, it might be somebody who is divorced or somebody who is in pre-foreclosure, or who is in foreclosure, obviously there is plenty of those today, but there are a number of different reasons why you find motivated sellers. Maybe it was grandma's house and she just passed away and the kids need to liquidate it to take care of her estate, there are a lot of different reasons. They are able to buy the $100,000 house for $60,000 and the house is obviously is not looking its best, maybe it hasn't been fixed up in quite some time, so they come in and buy the property for $60,000 and they put $20,000 into it to fix it up, and they have a cost basis of $80,000 the market value is $100,000 they go out to the market and they sell it for $95,000 let's say, so they made a $15,000 profit on that $60,000 deal. That is a 25% rate or return on you money, not too bad especially when it is secured by real estate, and again at all points there we are dealing with a property that we bought at below market value.

With an IRA the way that one would go about that is that they would find the deal, they would negotiate the terms over that $60,000 purchase price and what they would do is they can either call into their first class service team here at Equity Trust or they could do it online where they download our form it is called the direction of investment, and they would use the real estate direction of investment. That is basically a form you are going to tell us what you want to buy, you are going to tell us the property address, the place that you are going to purchase at, the title company that you are going to utilize, and basically when the deal is ready to close where you want us to send the money. So if it needs to go to an escrow account do you want us to send it to the title company or do you want us to send it by wire or check and so forth. It is a pretty simple form, straight forward, you let us know the investment that you want to buy, then we will work with the title company or the attorney, depending on the state, if they have title companies or not, and we will make sure all the paperwork is in proper order, you would go to a closing just like you would for your own property, but instead of you buying the property your IRA is going to be purchasing the property, the deal is going to close, the money will change hands and the deed will now be recorded in your IRAs name.

Okay.

Now with that the IRA owns the property, and the great part about that is again that any profit that is made on that property is all going to flow back to your IRA.

That is great. That is excellent. Like you are saying when it flows back into there it becomes tax deferred and you can simply keep reinvesting those monies and the future properties further on down the road, correct?

Exactly. When you really look at it and you say okay, let's say that you are an active investor and you are working a couple of neighborhoods in your area that you really know and you have your feelers out and you are looking for the deals, and let's say that you were able to do that 3 times,

3 times in a year so once every 4 months even twice a year, twice a year, you are doing 2 deals a year for your IRA forget the compounding interest, you are earning a 50% rate or return on your money.

You're IRA?

Exactly.

Safely, securely as well because it is a hard asset and again everybody needs a place to live in, so affordable housing and a very consistent manner it is always going to be there and as long as they educate themselves they will be okay, correct?

Exactly and again even with today's environment because you know rather than sell that house, why don't we turn it into a rental and have rental income. So if you want to go that route then you have a great opportunity there to obviously to have all of that rental income come back to the IRA and as the markets improve all of that appreciation, which is I kind of like to look at it as kind of icing on the cake, all is going to accumulate within the IRA. If we take this one step further, one step further since we have the property in our IRA and we use the IRA to buy it completely, you know a lot of people today are having trouble finding credit, right, going and getting a mortgage.

You do your due diligence and you get to know the people, good people maybe they lost their job and they got a new job, maybe they over extended themselves a bit, but really have never been late on payments before, whatever the reason might be, but if you want to really hit a home run then what you might do is sell that property, that property remember we had an $80,000 cost basis in it. We might sell it for $100,000, but we would do it with seller financing. Which is what we do is basically in exchange for the property, so I sell you the property for $100,000 and what does the IRA get back? The IRA gets back let's say, maybe 10% down, so $10,000 in cash and then it receives a note for $90,000. The note by itself, because of the credit crunch and because of whatever issues they might have had, the people who are buying the property, it might have a 10,12,15,18% rate of return. Now that is obviously something that you negotiate with each deal, but how would you like to have that? You basically built in and you have sold the house for $100,000 so you have already made your $20,000 and on top of it now you have a note that is paying you back at 10,12,15,18%. It is a home run and there are so many opportunities out there right now. That deal that I gave you is a pretty conservative one. Most investors that I talk to really wouldn't look at a deal or spend the time for under $25,000 or $30,000 in terms of profit, so in that one we are just talking 20% or $20.

That is great. I mean, again and this is why I like what you guys do at your company. I have called into your companies, I have done deals with your guys with IRAs in the past with clients of mine and what is grade A. Not only that Jeff, you guys do a great job educating your staff on how to handle questions, objectives because truthfully you guys are there for them. You

guys go above and beyond the call of duty in customer service and that is me because I have called in and I am a 100-question guy, so you guys work for us.

I appreciate that very much. We have an incredible staff here and you are exactly right. When we look at what kind of the mission of this company it is to help investors make tax-free profits, and we are here for our customers, we are not selling any products, any investments, we don't give any investment advice, we are here to help you get the deal done that you want to do.

Absolutely that is great. I do a lot of investing from across the border, right now I am in Atlanta, we have deals going on in Ohio, Illinois, Missouri, Michigan, Wisconsin, and Texas and we have people that do invest monies from outside of their state boundaries, like when they are using their IRA's they can invest it in any form they want? Correct, because I know you guys do promissory notes and other investments like this as well, correct?

Correct. Again we can handle clients from all 50 states and they can invest wherever they would like to and we can handle just kind of the top 5 or 6 investment vehicles if you will that people utilize is going to be real estate, there are going to be notes or when they are lending money and sometimes that is secured by real estate and we will call that a mortgage or a deed of trust, sometimes it is unsecured, sometimes it is secured by something other than real estate. Then when people often times will find private

Go Grab Your $247 of FREE Gifts at www.InsiderSecretsMoney.com

placement kind of investment opportunities, it might be somebody starting the community bank or a restaurant or a business in the area. There are so many opportunities to really customize this account to what fits your needs, and there is so much flexibility and that is probably the most powerful aspect of these accounts.

Yeah the flexibility you're referencing?

Exactly.

I think it is key anytime, like you said when you go into a real estate deal especially, I know that is not the only avenues you have accessibility to, but with real estate there are so many options available to you if you buy correctly. Like you said you could do a rental, you can do a lease option, you could do a sell and hold the mortgage, and accelerate the process and growth of your IRA by the more education you learn in real estate, the more knowledge you know and how to purchase real estate. There is so many ways to buy as you know and so it is just making sure that you have the time for it and if you don't find others that are willing to help you move forward, to educate you, and guide you the correct way so to speak.

Definitely. It is very important that we do things the right way.

Absolutely. With that said, with everything that is going on and because you know I educate investors, real estate investors all over the world, how do you see because I am always telling my clients the best way... because everybody is worried about we can't get loans, or we can't get this, or we can't do that and so really fine people educate them on how to tap into funds that are available today, they just might not even know that they exist, which is a lot of people and educate them and direct them your way and really provide a solution as opposed to a problem. That is what you guys do right; you provide the solution to access their capital?

Exactly, I mean what we are able to do is just open another door like you said of financing. It is really again across the board for real estate investors who are looking to sell investment properties or realtors; it is another avenue to go to. The people who have dealt with you before and say look you know if you have already bought a property from me and it has worked out well and you are looking to buy another, have you ever thought about using your IRA, and again obviously for investors doing for themselves the majority of people who are coming from corporate America have some funds in an IRA or a 401K and again for most of us when we make that transition it is really going well my money is in a plan with a company that I am no longer with, are they really looking out for my best interest and am I comfortable with leaving my money in the market versus having that freedom and really that access to capital to invest what I think is valuable or value added and a great opportunity.

Absolutely. What would you say to an investor because I am on a side where I hear it is just a mind set

shift with folks that have this money, the ones that don't educate themselves, they kind of act like that money doesn't even exist. What I always educate my guys is, I say look they are not looking to make a million dollars a day, they simply want something stable, secure, consistent, and no hassle. So when I have investors and I am educating them it is a huge pool and I don't even know how big the IRA funds are or how many millions or trillions or billions of dollars are acceptable, but there is a lot of access to this. I will talk to just Joe Shmo off the street and you will find out that they have $300,000 or $400,000 just sitting and it is just stagnant, they are so afraid to do anything with it because they don't know what to do.

Well that is very true, I mean it is not uncommon to come across individuals with $100,000, $200,000, $300,000 in their 401K just from working on the job for 15, 20, 25 years and accumulating and contributing. You made great points there where for many people and again it is to each and kind of their own comfort level, but many do kind of just look at it like well I can't really do anything with that, I really can't have any control over growing it and really assuring myself that when I can get access to that money that it is the size or the amount that I need. Especially now in the real estate market, you look at this and this is something we talk about all the time. You are looking at a market really that is at its lowest point in many, many years, and it is a great time to get into the market right now if you have cash to buy real estate. Now on the other hand you have people who have a good amount of cash locked up in their 401K or in their IRAs in a stock market that is really having its trouble right now and you kind of put the two together and say okay if you have a lot of cash you can get great deals in real estate right now, and you have a lot of cash locked up over here in this 401K how can I move that cash to an environment where I can activate it and start to take advantage of these great deals that you can get right now in real estate. That is what the self-directed IRA allows you to do.

That is great. There is so many ways and I could talk a hundred times about this because I get excited about this because it taps into a whole different source. What I love about times like this too Jeff is that you really start seeing the strong investors, the ones that really do commit to being successful in this business and creating new opportunities when maybe the door shuts on one kind of financing technique etc but it is really indulging yourself in the process of education, and knowing hey there are alternatives on what you can do about it. I don't want to cherry coat it though too much, but can you tell me about what kind of investments I can make and such, because I know the IRS does limit certain transactions, could you talk a little bit about that as well?

Sure. Well you know first off in terms of what you can and cannot do. Let's talk about three main areas and we kind of talk about the rules of what we can and cannot do. The first one is let's talk about prohibited investments or these are going to be assets that our IRA cannot buy with

Go Grab Your $247 of FREE Gifts at www.InsiderSecretsMoney.com

an IRA, and predominantly these are based around collectibles, artwork, rugs, gems, precious metals, alcoholic beverages like wine, so specifically the government says that we cannot purchase collectibles with our IRA. Beyond collectibles it really leaves it pretty open and gives us quite an array of investments obviously or assets to buy with the IRA. Real estate, mortgages, tax liens, mobile homes, these are all assets that your IRA can invest in.

Number two is we talked about prohibited investments, let's talk next about disqualified individuals, and these are people that our IRA cannot have business dealings with. Something that is very important to clarify right off the bat is the number one disqualified person with an IRA is yourself or the IRA account holder. What I mean by that is that your IRA cannot buy a property from yourself, so if you already own it personally, your IRA cannot buy that property from you. You can buy it from any third party in theory if you are out looking for deals in your neighborhood, but it just can't buy a property that you already own. There are a number of disqualified people or again people that your IRA cannot do business with, and again it starts with yourself as number one and then the second group is family members of linear decent. What we mean by linear decent is basically grandparents, parents, spouse, children, and grandchildren. What it does not include are aunts and uncles, nieces and nephews, brothers and sisters, business associates, partners, friends, those are all people that you can do business with your IRA. But then again that family members of linear decent the grandparents, parents, spouse, children and grandchildren, and the IRA owner themselves, those are disqualified individuals or people that our IRA cannot have business dealings with.

When I talk about business dealings it is kind of a good transition into the third area of rules that we should cover and that is prohibited transactions, it is kind of the third grouping. Prohibited transactions are basically business dealings that our IRA cannot be involved with. The first one that I had already mentioned is basically buying an investment from a disqualified individual. Again, you cannot buy that piece of property that your mom owns, or your grandparents own, or you can't sell a property from your IRA to your child, but you can buy a property from again any third party that is out there that you come across with negotiating property, you could buy a property from a business partner or from a friend, but just not from those disqualified individuals.

There are a number of prohibited transactions and the main ones are again number one is you can't buy a property or sell a property to a disqualified person. You cannot loan money from your IRA to a disqualified person, so I can't lend money from my IRA to again my grandchild, but I could lend money to anyone who is not a disqualified individual.

Okay.

I can't buy a property with my IRA for personal use. If you buy a vacation property and we have a lot of clients who will buy property on the ocean and they will rent that property out and obviously the IRAs collect all that rental income but you and or any other disqualified individual cannot use that rental property anytime throughout the year because we have to really remain focused and remember that our IRAs are buying these properties for an investment, they are not buying it for any type of personal use.

Just to kind of recap, again when we talk about what we can and cannot do there I'd really like to talk about three main areas. Our prohibited investments, we cannot buy with our IRA, which are mainly collectibles, disqualified individuals which for our audience basically includes family members of linear decent and ourselves as the IRA owner and then the third grouping is those prohibited transactions, again business dealings that our IRA cannot be involved with.

But again Mark I think the most important thing that I can make about these rules is that for 99% of our clients who are going out and buying property day in and day out, just like they would if the IRA wasn't there, they are buying in the deals, they are negotiating them, they are using flyers, they have bird dogs, however they are finding these deals, 99% of them is a very simple straight forward transaction because they are not dealing with family members or trying to make a deal happen that really isn't one that they have come across as an investor. So for the vast majority it is pretty straightforward and pretty black and white.

That is excellent. I appreciate that. I mean we are hearing about everything you guys have going Jeff.

Can you give us a little bit of a brief history behind you guys? We have heard what he is saying and everything, but what gives them the right to say these kind of things and kind of the authority position correct, can you tell us a little bit about that because it is excellent.

Yes definitely and it is a great story. My father started the company back in 1974 and at that time he had started. Actually, before that I worked at a brokerage firm as a stockbroker and very successful salesman and branch manager and did very well and had a great mentor who said you know what you really should go out on your own and you should start your own business, you know you have the talent and the ability and I will help you with the capital, so let's make it happen. So in 1974 he started his own firm, and again it was plain vanilla kind of brokerage firm you know come in off the street and buy a hundred shares of IBM. My father really since 1965 has been a real estate investor, and he started off with single family homes and duplexes, and decided in the late 70's that the stock market was great, but when the market was down nobody was buying and as a commission only stock broker like they used to be, if people aren't buying you are not making any money. So he really needed to be able to kind of insure that he could have a steady flow of income and really work on multiple fronts, so he moved from single family homes and duplexes to commercial buildings, shopping centers, office buildings, and so forth and so he started to put together private placements here in our local area. This was basically in 1981, 1982 and he recognized at that time he said wow these IRA's though they just came about a couple of years ago at that time, these things are going to be powerful and they are a great funding source for my deals. I can get 20, 30, 40 people together and they can all put in $5,000 or $10,000 from their IRA's because they were smaller back then and now I got a couple hundred thousand dollars that we can put together a deal and bring a tenant in and really provide a great rate of return.

He went to the couple of firms that were offering this flexibility back then and really found out pretty quickly that they were not easy to do business with, they were all across the country and obviously this before fax and e-mail, and he said you know what, we have a brokerage firm we should be able to do this ourselves, act as custodian and facilitate these transactions. He said I know real estate I do this day in and day out and I understand the brokerage end so why can't I put these two together, and so we went through in 1982 the almost year long process to be approved by the IRS to be able to handle these types of IRA's and in 1983 I am proud to say that I think we were the 63rd or maybe 64th company in the entire country that was able to do this. We have been in the game for quite some time now.

Basically it started with that first deal and from that first deal somebody said to my father you know this is great that I can invest it in real estate, can I buy a property in Texas, and he said I don't know. I don't know if you can buy one in Texas, let me go to the attorneys and we went though it and found out yeah you can buy property in Texas and in fact in all 50 states, and it really snowballed from there where that person used their IRA and then more people from Texas said okay I want to buy similar properties and then it went to Florida. It is a great story because my father is really a true entrepreneur and it is one of those great stories where there was no grand plan, no kind of MBA to get this business going, but it was more of kind of creating it for our own needs and kind of stumbling upon this demand that all these other people needed too. So I am proud to say really since 1974 we have been involved with IRA's and obviously the financial service business and since 83 we have seen growth every single year since, and every year just gets bigger and bigger and bigger.

That is excellent I appreciate that. Can you talk about and I don't know if you want to reveal this, but kind of like with Equity Trust do you guys talk about how much funds are in your area that you guy see daily, it is probably such a high number most people won't even fathom it correct?

Exactly. I mean in terms of the assets that we act as custodian for it is in the billions of dollars and on a weekly basis I would have to imagine easily, easily in terms of just changing back and forth 40, 50, 60 million dollars a week, we are doing 600 deals a week and most of those are real estate related so we are going ahead and doing closings all the time all across the country. People are paying bills they are getting rental income, they are selling properties, so we have a fine tune machine here we have over 180 employees that go through extensive training that can help our clients and we are focused on one thing and I like to think that we might not be able to do a lot of things great, but we can do a few things great, and we stay focused, we stay focused on helping our clients make money and really understanding the IRAs and how people are utilizing them.

That is excellent. Not only that what that does is when you do stay focused which all successful business are focused is it really gives you time to create better solutions as times change, because it is always changes there is always change going on and it is how can I provide more value, how can this be simpler, how can this be more streamlined right in your own business.

Exactly and that is something that we really stress on, actually that is kind of our number one core value is we are innovators and we are constantly looking for better ways to make these transactions flow. We obviously follow the rules that are set by the government so we just can't make up our own rules, but as long as we stay within the confines of what the government has told us we need to do, we really just constantly look for a better way.

Absolutely. Not only that but really quick if I could extract back again, you just said you do about 600 transactions a week with 30, 40, 50 million dollars a week. The reason I like that I think a lot of people especially as me as an entrepreneur and business owner and investor is sometimes we feel like we are like by ourselves or alone, and the thing is we are not there is a lot of people out here doing it just not maybe not talking about it like you and I, but really there is so much opportunity and

you don't have to recreate the wheel.

Exactly. I mean that is so true and there are so many investors that are out there and that is one of the things that we really pride ourselves on is Equity Trust really tries to provide opportunities for investors to get together to talk and to really learn from each other, because there are thousands tens of thousands of equity trust company clients that are out there actively involved in the market. We do that through live events, we offer one day events where we travel all across the country and we provide our clients the opportunity to spend a day with us, we do multi day events and we have conference calls that client can be on and ask questions where we bring in experts in different investing fields as well as the clients that are hitting home runs right now, so in addition to acting as a custodian, kind of doing the paperwork which we are very focused on and we take that very seriously. As I kind of started the call we really look at ourselves as a custodian but we are really here to help our clients be successful, and so part of it is handling acting as custodian and administrator, part of it is education, and helping out clients understand what their options are and then the third component is really again creating a forum or community where our clients can learn from each other as well as ourselves and really that is just a great combination that people are looking for and it really is invaluable.

Absolutely. Now we know with what is going on out there right now you guys you know there are other companies that try to pop up and try to imitate all that stuff

out there. **Jeff can you talk a little bit about this because I know your guys of core concepts is huge and it is very strong and great companies have a great core. Can you talk a little bit about that here?**

Sure well you know again there are other companies that are in the market place and by enlarge what we like to do is talk about who we are and our story and what we offer and allow our clients to make that decision on their own, but it is very important to us again that if you were to ask again the majority of companies in the industry, if you said what do you do again they are going to say we are an administrator, we push paper. Well we are not. We are committed to our clients success and working with them. I think from the start that really kind of shows our position and where our future and our strategic initiatives are focused, and that is helping our clients become more successful.

Number one is having been in business sine 1974 is obviously very important over 35 years or basically 35 years. Well the way we like to look at it is that if you are making telephones for calculators or cars for that matter, to be in business for 35 years means that you are doing something right. Obviously for all those 35 years we are in a highly regulated industry so we have government oversight and that is very important because not all companies in our industry have the same level of government oversight, and again when making a decision on a financial services firm it is very important to look at their track record and to understand who is watching your money when you are not. Obviously our size and our client base with close to 45,000 clients, again in all 50 states and 13 foreign countries is very important to us, and then our people, our people really they are the ones who make us who we are. We have approximately 180 employees here that are well trained, focused on helping our clients be more successful, and get to where they want to be.

Most of our employees receive a considerable amount of education and training when they are hired. All employees receive one hour of continuing education every single week, so that training is there again focus on how do we make our clients life easier. I think that is really important that customers realize again that our focus is how do we make your lives easier and how do we help you become more successful. Our core values it resonates through all of them, it resonates through taking care of our customer, providing the best possible product, giving them the most flexibility and the most tools that can help them be successful, and really be their partner and that is what we do.

That is great. I know from personal experience I have used two other companies out there prior to knowing about you guys and now I have everybody move over, but the simplicity and the knowledge base that you guys like you said because you do care is so much stronger and internally and it is a core that everybody is on the same page, and with those other companies I mean you would call one person and they wouldn't know what the left hand and the right hand was doing, they had no clue. So it is really good you guys really have had it locked down and the dedication I didn't know you guys

did an hour a week which is excellent.

It definitely it is just one component that and obviously when it comes to our fee schedule, we keep it very simple for our customers. We are the only company really in the industry that has an all inclusive fee schedule, and what that means is our clients pay one fee at the beginning of the year and it includes all of their transactions. So no matter how many investments you want to buy yourself, how many checks you need, how many times you call us for information; it is all included we keep it very simple. I mean a $100,000 account is $350, $200,000 is $350 dollars a year, so it is very reasonable and again we keep it simple and not try to nickel and dime our clients.

Exactly and I think that is super important. So real quick, here's a couple more questions here Jeff before we let you go. With what you guys have going on and we kind of talked about this why the clients do choose you and the recommendations and I know when I wanted to get you to do this book I spoke to Brad and I was like I can't do it with anybody else, he has got to make time for this because I won't recommend anybody else. It just holds true to my fact, but the other people I know I am assuming they are experiencing the same results that I am getting with your company as well, right?

Definitely. It is really important to us as we said it is obviously taking care of our customer and we have a continuous survey program that allows our clients after transactions to be able to tell us how we are doing, what can we do better, and that is a very important score that we share throughout the entire company and we are very happy with where our scores are at and obviously always looking for ways to improve. Our biggest growth source has been from client referrals and it is our life blood, we are very appreciative of it, and we recognize again that if we can provide a great product at a reasonable price and take care of our customers the growth and the money follows and so we stay focused on that.

I know we are talking about IRAs and self-directed IRAs I should say, but truthfully this is really business 101, and on top of what you guys do as well. I see a lot of times business folks they get so consumed and again I think it streams right back to the core of stay focused.

Definitely.

That is great. I guess a couple more things here. Where do you see the new direction, where do you see direction with Equity Trust Company, where do you guys see yourself in the next couple of years, and I also just thought about this, but isn't there something coming out in 2010 that the clients might be able to benefit from?

Definitely. There are a couple of things but with 2010 let's talk about that real quick. It is a very important date we have been talking about it for quite some time now and in our education forums because we really want our customers to recognize the power and it is just starting to pick up some steam now, but in 2010 what the government is going to allow us to do is they are going to allow you to convert your traditional IRA or any tax deferred IRA to a tax-free ROTH IRA, and that is a huge opportunity.

Right now it is basically capped at if you are single or you are married and file jointly if you make over $100,000 a year you do not have the right to convert from a traditional IRA to a ROTH IRA. So many Americans obviously are not able to take advantage of that. In 2010 the government is saying for 1 year we are going to allow anybody who wants to convert their traditional IRA's to a ROTH, and we are going to give you two years to take care of the taxes that will apply. So you can spread the taxes out over two years this is a huge opportunity because obviously one of our famous sayings in our education is would you rather pay tax on the seed or on the crop. If you have a $100,000 account today, would you rather pay taxes on $100,000 today or on a million dollars 10 or 15 years from now. Obviously let's take care of it today, let's move that account from that $100,000 account from a taxable account or tax-deferred, excuse me to a tax-free account where you will never pay income tax on the qualified distribution ever again. It is huge, so when you become a client of Equity Trust you also get exposed to our great ideas, strategies, and concepts that you really need to be aware of to make the right decisions. That is just one example of a great situation that every investor should be aware of.

Absolutely that is excellent. Real quick I have a question if they transfer that $100,000 let's use the seed concept again, if they transfer that $100,000 they pay

the tax ramifications for those next two years correct they could spread it out over two years?

Yes.

Then once that gets spread out now what they are able to do is now the money that is coming into the system into their self-directed IRA is not tax-deferred it is tax-free?

Correct because it is really what we should have mentioned a little bit earlier. There is basically two types of accounts, there is tax-deferred and tax-free and the tax deferred basically means is that when you put money in or when you make contributions to your IRA if it is a tax-deferred account you are going to receive in most cases a deduction when you put the money in, so you can write that off on your taxes. So you put money in you get a write off and you are able to invest it in real estate stock, however you want it throughout the life of the account, and then once you reach the age of 59-1/2 you can start taking money out, and at that point with a tax-deferred account when you start to take money out you are going to have to pay ordinary income tax at that point in time. With the ROTH or the tax-free account it kind of works the opposite. When you put money in or you make contributions you are not going to receive a deduction and that is going to be on those contributions…you are going to be happy to pay those taxes, you want to pay the tax to get that 4 or 5 thousand dollars in the account because once that becomes ROTH money those are tax-free dollars. What I mean by that is as you start to make investments and you grow that account, once you reach the age of 59-1/2 and you have had your ROTH open for at least 5 years, once you have met those two requirements you now have the ability to pull that money out of your ROTH IRA completely income tax free for the rest of your life, your spouse's life and your beneficiaries life, so that could grow for over a hundred years without any taxes, it is incredible.

Yeah that is incredible. That is a whole other book in itself, but that is an excellent, excellent opportunity for anybody that is serious about really wanting to grow future wealth, it is so powerful. Okay Jeff, well cool man I don't know do you have a web site or something you would like to give for people to come out and take a look and learn more about Equity Trust Company and learn more about you as a person and kind of go from there?

Definitely. Our website is **www.trustetc.com** so it is basically trust equity trust company.com **www.trustetc.com** and on the site because we have a lot of great information, education, opportunities for people who are looking at the IRAs to learn more and to get exposed to some of these great ideas and I would highly suggest that you sign up for some of our great reports. We have news feeds that we can provide to you as well, and then really we talk about our great people and our great trained people, we have an incredible staff that can help you understand what accounts are out there for you and what might be the best fit and really to answer all of your questions as it relates to getting started and making that first investment. From the site you can give us a call, you can get all of our information, or if you want to do an online chat you can do that as well. I would definitely say visit the site, there is a lot of great information and make the call. Give us a call and the rest from there we can help you and it is really downhill after you make that first phone call.

That is excellent. Well thank you Jeff for your time, and have a great day.

All right great, thanks a lot Mark.

Thanks Jeff.

Chapter Three
Interview with Lee Arnold

We have an amazing guest on today's call that is going to be dissecting the private money market for you, and letting you know how you can use that to leverage your business as a real estate investor. The gentleman that we have here is a marketing real estate entrepreneur.

Lee has quickly redefined the role, and definitely broken the mold of the common-place guru. Starting from meager beginnings, he's swiftly launched himself into the company of multi-millionaires at a very young age.

With his easily integrated marketing methods and real estate strategies, he has helped others achieve the same type of success and financial freedom, and he hasn't stopped there. With each passing year, Lee continues to crack the code to financial success.

Recently featured in *Forbes*, *The Boston Globe*, *Market Watch*, *Business Week*, and *Reuters* as a leading foreclosure expert, Lee Arnold has made a personal fortune in investing and real estate, and specifically in loan modification, short sale, private money, private money refinancing, and foreclosure transactions.

With years and years of "practice makes perfect," he has mastered the fine art of real estate investing—a national speaker and renowned author, Lee has armed thousands of real estate investors with these hard-earned secrets and time-tested strategies. Lee, welcome to the call.

Hey, thanks for having me here today. I'm happy to be here.

Perfect. I'm excited to have you. I know with private money being a very big topic, especially in today's challenges, it's going to be an amazing content for our readers and listeners to go ahead and learn a lot of these great strategies.

Let's go ahead and jump right into it. Why don't you go ahead and give us a briefing of what private money is.

Okay. Private money is money that is held by private individuals not institutions or conventional lenders.

These are people who have 401K's or IRA's or money in retirement or investment accounts that are earning 2 or 3% and they would like to earn 6 or 7 or 8%. So it's anybody that's got some cash lying around that they would like to put into a safe investment that's going to give them a greater return than they are currently getting.

Okay. With that being said, how does that actually differ from hard money?

Private money is different. It's very different, mainly because private money typically doesn't have the same background as hard money. Hard money in fact is usually money that's being brokered from private individuals by people who are in the business—mortgage companies, banks. They go out and find these individuals and then they lend it out to other investors.

The fine line really comes down to cost. Private money, if you know how to negotiate it in the right way, you know the pockets to go and get it, and you can usually tie it up for 6 or 7 or 8% interest.

Whereas a hard money lender, they have gone out and found the private money individual, and they are going to charge you four or five points, sometimes higher in some cases, and they are going to mark it up to 15 or 20% interest.

So the hard money lender essentially is borrowing the private money, brokering it to the end-user, or the investor that needs it for their development project or their investment opportunity, and the middleman, the broker, is going to make 8 to 15 points on the spread.

If you can take these private money concepts and go find these individuals with these pocket monies yourself, you're going to save yourself a substantial amount of money. Hard money lenders typically (and I hate to use the word "prey" because I don't want to evoke that word's imagery), but people who borrow hard money typically don't understand the lending world very well.

So, definitely, it sounds like private money is a great avenue for them, but with that said why is private money necessary in today's economy?

With the mortgage meltdown and the banking debacle and everything that's gone on the last 12 and 24 months, institutional lenders, i.e. banks, Wall Street, hedge funds, pension plans, they've gotten pretty skittish as to who they are willing to lend money to, and as a result the financial and credit required credentials to get institutional and conventional money are almost impossible to come by.

I've got a lot of friends that going through the real estate meltdown, I mean they literally lost millions and millions of dollars in their personal portfolio from real estate devaluation, and rather than throwing good money after bad debt, many of them opted to just do a short sale or to let the property revert back to the lender, which of course resulted in them having a horrible credit rating.

It's these people, it's these individuals, who in my opinion make the world turn because they are the ones going out and identifying raw pieces of ground that will make great shopping centers and good development opportunities and a nice subdivision for housing, but these individuals can no longer go out and borrow money from conventional or institutional lenders because they are too afraid to give those folks money.

If the economy is going to turn around at all, we have to get money back into the hands of the entrepreneurs.

We can't continue to give money to big banks because big banks aren't giving it out to anyone else.

We can't continue to give it out to the poor and the middle class because they are not going to create industry. They are not going to take those funds and go out and start companies that now need employees and produce products that we can then ship overseas and manufacture and beef up our GDP.

So we've got to get cash into the hands of the people that know how to make money with it.

Unfortunately, banks look at people who had some challenges over the last couple of years because they were running their businesses at such an amazing level that they no longer give you funding.

For example, I've got a friend, actually a partner of mine; we were doing some development in the Park City, Utah, area. We had some really beautiful, ski in, ski out homes, and my partner when I met him back in '05 had a net worth of $1.5 billion.

He was building 10,000 houses a year in the Sacramento Valley and all around California and Phoenix and Nevada. I mean this guy was employing literally thousands of people like subcontractors. He was really creating an amazing liquidity in the market place.

When the market turned for him in California in '07, he found himself going from a $1.5 billion net worth to a negative $400 million upside-down situation, at which point a ton of houses went into foreclosure, he got sued, deficiency judgments, garnishments and all these things.

Well, he still has all that knowledge, and now you can go out and buy land for 10 cents on the dollar for what he was buying it for back in '05 and '06, so he still has all the knowledge that he can go out and create industry, create jobs, create manufacturing, which will boost up the financial system, but nobody will give him any money to do it.

So the only place he's going to be able to find the people who will give him cash is in the private money sector, and in my opinion, right now, there is more money in the private sector than we have ever seen because even private money individuals are afraid to give it to institutions.

They don't want to give it to Wall Street because they are afraid Wall Street's going to give it to guys like Bernie Madoff. So the entire system is scared, and scared money is attracted by sound projects and sound opportunity, and there are so many good projects because you literally can get great deals all over the country right now.

I'm in the process of reading a book right now called, <u>America for Sale</u> by Jerome Corsi, PhD, great book, and he's dead right. America is for sale, and if you've got cash liquidity or a great idea, you can get funding.

Yes, definitely. And I imagine these people, these private lenders, would want to have their investments secured somehow, so how is private money secured? Is it just real estate, or are there other assets that can be collateralized?

Well, there are two ways to collateralize funding—either through real property or through real assets. And in today's market, assets can be considered either inventory, assets can be merchant accounts, monies that are coming in. Assets can be accounts receivable.

Go Grab Your $247 of FREE Gifts at www.InsiderSecretsMoney.com

And this is really getting into the factoring side of business, so in the private money world, if you are lending against receivables or other assets within the company or organization, you are really doing what's called factoring, and there is a substantial amount of money out there for factoring.

However, the easier money is when you secure it against real property so if there is a piece of real estate that's involved in the transaction, funding is going to be much easier to come by, so you can either secure it in one or two ways.

Now that is on existing structures, and I'll tell you the easiest deals to get funding on are large commercial projects. And when I say large I'm talking about bigger than $5 million, where there's already an existing cash flow.

So for example, if you could go out and find an apartment building, let's call it a 100-unit apartment building, that you can pick up for 5000 bucks per door, or $5 million, that's a very easy loan to get assuming that 50% of the units of that building are churning cash.

And what's fascinating about private money is that anybody can identify private money and you can go out and get private money whether you've got cash or not, as long as you've identified the opportunity.

Because like I said, the private money follows the opportunity, and a 100-unit apartment building for $5,000 a door is an amazing opportunity assuming that it's churning

Go Grab Your $247 of FREE Gifts at www.InsiderSecretsMoney.com

out 500 bucks a unit, that would be half a million dollars a month. That's not a bad deal. Actually, I'm sorry that's $50,000 a month, but still a great return on investment.

So that's what private money is looking for right now—existing structures. Private money is not real interested in development right now because development is still a little "what if." But an existing building that's churning out cash flow is very, very easy to get funding and very easy to secure and collateralize.

As you mentioned, you think there is more private money out there now than has ever been available to us, or has been available in a long time, so how would someone go out and locate private money?

Private money is actually in some areas easier to spot than others, and if you've read The Millionaire Next Door, it's a fascinating book because The Millionaire Next Door talks about the average American millionaire. They aren't flashy; they don't live in big houses.

If you look at Warren Buffett, he's still living in the same little 2,200 square foot for the last forty years. He's the richest man in America, and he's still living that lifestyle. So people need to understand that the "millionaire next door" doesn't mean Rolls Royce, flashy cars, big rings, and those types of things. Typically that's surface wealth.

So to identify private money, you want to go into not surface wealth, but you want to identify people who have wealth in depth, meaning they have been established in their career for quite some time, they are living on the same property for quite some time. And the easiest way to track them down, interestingly enough, is through public records.

In public records, you can pull up every property in America that is owned free and clear, and for the "millionaire next door," 99% of them own their home free and clear. So if you pull public record on a half-million dollar property and they owe nothing against it, that's a half-million dollar asset that they could borrow against if they needed to, or wanted to, to put money into a project.

Now that usually won't be the case, because if they own their home free and clear, they are probably sitting on several hundred thousand, if not several million dollars in liquidity in some retirement account, or some pension plan, or some 401K or IRA.

So the easiest place to find private money is just by tracking homes that are paid for free and clear, and most people aren't aware that in America, even in today's economy, in America today, 30% of housing is owned free and clear.

That's definitely an amazing tip and strategy. I appreciate that. Here is a quick question. How quickly can the average person identify a private money lender when needing funds or brokering funds?

Okay.

I might be ahead of myself with a brokering fund, but...

I want to start with this. Getting into the industry or identifying private money is actually the exact opposite of how you would think you would go about it. And what I mean by that is you don't actually go out in search of private money lenders until you've identified an opportunity.

People's time would be much better spent going out and finding that 100-unit apartment building and putting it under contract for $5 million, and then going in search of the private money because as I mentioned before money follows opportunity. Money very rarely follows people.

Even some of the most successful entrepreneurs out there, if they would just start calling all their friends saying, "Hey, give me a million bucks." And they go, "For what?" "Well, I don't know. I'm going to find something." That's typically not how it works.

Most successful, wealthy entrepreneurs do not go in search of funding until they've identified the opportunity. And even to this day I'm the same way. I will not employee my private money pools that I have identified until I have something to bring to them.

So for people who either need private money because they've already established the opportunity, or people who want to broker private money, the first step is identifying that great deal. And then here's the key, you've got to have a great deal under contract.

It's amazing the number of calls I get in any given week from people going, "Hey, will you lend me $100,000?"

"For what?"

"Well, I've got this opportunity over here on the west side, and I think it'd be good."

"Do you have it under contract?"

"Well, no."

"So right now while you're talking to me, another investor could be over there talking to the seller tying that deal up."

So it's more than just identifying the opportunity, it's tying up the opportunity by putting it under contract. Then you go in search of the private money. And once you have that, the private money is very easy to find.

You know with that said, there's a thing out there called transactional funding that a lot of people are talking about, and it's becoming bigger and bigger. How does transactional funding actually differentiate from private funds?

Transactional funding is used for a very short periods of time. So for example, let's say that I've identified the $5 million apartment building, and I need to close on my end because we can no longer do what's called a double-close or double-contracting. Years and years ago you used to be able to buy that $5 million apartment building with the person's money that I sold it to.

So, Nate, let's take you. I've identified a $5 million dollar apartment building. I then identify you, Nate, and you're

Go Grab Your $247 of FREE Gifts at www.InsiderSecretsMoney.com

willing to buy that apartment building from me for $6 million dollars. So I contract with you. You go out and you find a lender who will give you the $6 million, and then I use your funds to close my side with the seller. This was a double-closing. Other areas refer to it as double-contracting.

We can't do that any more. Title companies, money lenders, everyone requires that before we can resell it to the next person, we have to take title to it. Well, the only way we can take title to is by closing escrow and by providing the funds necessary to do that.

So in that scenario, Nate, if I've identified you, I will go get a transactional funding (a transactional lender) to give me money for 24 or 36 hours which will allow me to close my side, put title to the building in my name at $5 million, and then, Nate, I'll sell it to you the next day, or the day after for the $6 million, and I'll just net the spread.

So transactional funding is very short term. It typically does not come with an interest rate. It only comes with a fee associated with it, and that fee is usually defined in the form of points, so transactional funding is going to run you anywhere from 2 to 5 points for that 24- or 72-hour period of time. Private money on the other hand can be anywhere from 2 or 3 days to 2 or 3 years.

Now certainly private money can be longer than three years, but that sweet spot is somewhere between 6 months and three years. That's where most private lenders want to be. They don't want to tie up their money for a longer period of time than that.

Private money lenders typically are used to parameters, such as a CD, where you'll put your money into a bank CD for up to 6 months at a certain fixed rate, where you are guaranteed a return and then you can get access to it again.

So because private money lenders are geared in that mind-frame, or that mentality, they want loans that are 6-36 months. They want to know that their money is going to be sitting there drawing them 8, 9, 10% interest for a good period of time.

That's the very long version. The short version is this: transactional money is short term; private money is a little longer term.

So transaction funding is one type of exit strategy—buy and sell fast?

Yes.

With private money you're obviously going to have a little different exit strategy. So with that, when you borrow private money, how do you go about determining your exit strategy to repay it?

And that's the question of the day. That is the great question, and for me, I could sit here for hours and give you 29 different ways that you could enter and exit a transaction, but I don't like to do that.

For me, I like to let the property decide what the exit strategy is. So if I acquire a piece of property, I either have in mind that I'm going to fix it up, clean it up, get the rent rolls up, and then resell it; or I'm going to buy it, hold it for a period of time and use it as a cash flow property; or I'm going to acquire it, portfolio it, and then leverage it for liquidity so I can finance it.

But there are a lot of strategies out there. So for me, I'm going to let the building decide. If I can get it under contract for $5 million, I'm immediately going to start marketing it, and if I can find a buyer that's willing to pay me $6 million in the next couple of days, then I'm probably going to flip it.

If I can't, $5 million is still a great buy. I'm probably then going to go in and see about buying it, cleaning it up, and reselling it for—let's say $9 or 10 million. And if that doesn't work, if I can't find a buyer at $9 or 10 million, then I'll probably go ahead and buy it, fix it up, and then I'll rent it out as cash flow, while I keep it for sale.

A lot of investors get into an investment opportunity on the front-end thinking, "I'm going to buy it and flip it." And in today's market, and in any market for that matter, that's not the best strategy.

If the house won't sell, you've got to have an option to be able to keep it, and hold it long term and rent it out, or you need to buy it at such a reduced price that there's enough marginal spread there that you can unload it at a low, low price point and still come out okay. So the property will determine that.

The key is that from the time that you lock it up under contract, meaning you control the deal and nobody can take the deal from you without giving you money, start marketing the property in all different ways—from wholesale investor opportunity where we want other investors who would like to acquire it, fix it up, clean it up, and we can just flip it to them.

And if that doesn't work, then market it for tenants. We need to fill it up. We need to get the occupancy up—get the rent rolls up.

Or market it to an end-user. "Hey, a 100-unit apartment building completely remodeled--$10 million."

Run all those ads at the same time, and just see what ads you get the most activity on. And then plan that to be your exit strategy.

Leading in to the private money, does somebody have to have good credit or excellent credit to go ahead and qualify for this type of transaction?

No. And that's what I love about private money. Remember private money doesn't follow people, private money follows opportunity.

The ability to find an opportunity doesn't mean that you've got good or bad credit. It just means that you've got a skill set that you to understand where good opportunities lie and you know how to go out and get them. So that's the direction we want people to go. In other words, don't worry about your credit.

That's the beauty of private money. I don't care if you were worth $1.5 billion two years ago and you've lost everything. You still have a propensity for finding great deals. And when you find them money will be available.

The benchmark is you need to be around 50 or 55 cents on the dollar of what the property is worth in it's current condition.

A lot of investors will go out and say, "Well, the property is worth $10 million fixed up, and I'm getting it for $5 million," which sounds like a really great deal. But if the property in it's current condition is only worth $5 million and you're getting it for $5 million, you're going to have to have some skin in the game.

You want to identify opportunities that represent low risk to the person who's going to put up the funding. Credit only becomes a requirement when the risk gets higher in the transaction. So the lower the risk the easier it's going to be to find private funds.

And with that said, there's a lot of different—you mentioned earlier—that obviously credit doesn't matter by there are a lot of different ways to structure deals or start your exit strategies. Something I've heard people talk about is cashing out at closing. Is it possible for a borrower of private money to go ahead and get cash at the closing?

Go Grab Your $247 of FREE Gifts at www.InsiderSecretsMoney.com

The short answer is "Yes, it is."

The more detailed answer is that it's got to be a really, really good deal. And it's not like you're going to leave closing with a big check so you can go out and spend it on whatever you want. Typically, cash at a closing is going to come in the form of an escrow where funds will be set aside and earmarked for a specific task.

So again using our $5 million dollar apartment building as the example, if the $5 million dollar apartment building will be worth $10 or 12 million fixed up, and it's going to take $1 million to fix it up, could you get a private money-lender to lend you $6 million--$5 million for acquisition and $1 million for fix-up and repair?

The answer is: Yes, but you're not going to leave closing with a million bucks. Funds would be earmarked and then you would be able to draw down against them based on a line-item draw-down.

It's very much like new construction where you're given $25,000 for footings and foundation; you're given $50,000 for pouring foundation walls, and on and on and on. So in a renovation project like that, you would create a line-item draw sheet and then escrow funds would be put up. Now that's on the real estate side.

If we are going over the factoring side where you're putting up accounts receivable or inventory or merchant account monies that are waiting to be deposited, in that scenario, you can get up to 65 cents on the dollar of those assets and those receivables in a cash-out fashion.

So if you've got $100,000 a month in receivables and only $30,000 in costs, you could borrow $65,000 against your $100,000 receivables for that month. $30,000 would go to pay off the underlying debts, and you could leave with $35,000 in cash. So on the factoring side: Yes, you can leave with a cashier's check.

On the real estate side, although it is possible, it's not very common.

Okay, so depending on the transaction type.

Yes.

Okay. Now we mentioned that you don't have to have credit, and a lot of people think they don't need any money whatsoever, but actually you might have to have some skin in the game, depending upon the size of the transaction, but can you actually get private money if you don't have any cash and credit? Can you still qualify for these types of loans?

Again the short answer is: Yes.

The longer qualified answer is: With most private money lenders, especially if you are new to this and you don't have a reputation for these types of transactions or these types of scenarios, a private money lender is going to want to see some skin in the game; but where a lot of new investors, especially, get caught up in that is when they think that skin in the game means me—I've personally got to be writing checks.

Skin in the game can come in the form of someone else infusing capital for you, so if you've got a rich uncle or something that's willing to put up a half-million bucks that can be your skin in the game.

Or if you've got a building that you own free and clear, you could put that up in what we call a cross-collateralization, where you're putting up another asset to buy down the risk associated with that new opportunity that the private lender would then collateralize both projects so that they were very, very well protected.

And that's really what it comes down to is private money is easy, but it also wants to be relatively low risk. So even though skin in the game from you isn't necessary, you're going to find that a majority of the time, the investor is going to want to see some infusion of capital or assets from somewhere or something.

The only qualifier on that is that it cannot be a personal residence, so you can't be putting up your own house as collateral on one of these types of loans because they won't do it. It's got to be investment project, or it's got to be a business that you own or control that you can collateralize and put up as collateral.

The private money lenders are looking for collateral or they're looking for a little bit of skin in the game, obviously that can differ and that can change depending on what the situation is. But with that said, what are

they looking to lend on? There are so many different kinds of deals out there. **So what are private lenders looking to lend on, and what is the actual success ratio for getting these types of loans?**

That's the thing I love more than anything about private money—is that private money is not discriminating to any individual deal.

It's only discriminating by the individual investor, so when you consider the millions and millions of people just in the U.S. that own their home free and clear, that have great retirement accounts, that have millions of dollars sitting in the bank or in a retirement account somewhere—when you consider the millions of people that that represents, you're not going to find one investor who is interested in lending in all areas.

You will most likely find that private money is specific to its own comfort niche, if you will. For example, if somebody comes to me and says, "Lee, I've got a manufacturing company, and we manufacture—let's call it cattle feed. So we've got this farmer and he manufactures cattle feed and he needs a $3 million loan to carry him through the harvest, and then at the end of the harvest he can pay off the loan.

Well, that loan—I'm going to be hard pressed to get funding on that scenario from a guy out of Southern California who's used to buying large apartment buildings. So that's not a good match for that particular loan.

Now just because I go to the guy in California who says

no to the loan, doesn't mean that it's not a great opportunity. It means that I haven't found the right money lender that is comfortable lending in that niche. The lender who is going to be interested in that niche is probably going to be a retired farmer.

So I'm going to take that particular opportunity to the Midwestern retired farmer, which is a very easy list to come by because they subscribe to magazines like *Farmers Monthly* or *Agricultural News*. It's a very easy market to identify.

That's what I love about private month is whatever the deal is, there is a subset category of wealthy individuals that I can very easily tap into once I have that opportunity.

So that $3 million loan for that farmer that's manufacturing cattle feed is very, very easy to place, because I've got an amazing opportunity and I know immediately where to take that opportunity.

And that's what's great about private money—if you get a no from this person, and that person, and the next person, and the next person, it doesn't mean that you don't have a good deal. It just means that you haven't found the right lender who is comfortable in investing in that particular niche market space, and we've seen this all over the place.

It was Microsoft—Bill Gates—he took his presentation to 43 different venture capital firms before one of them said yes. So it's important especially for people who are new to this side of the business, or just looking to get started.

It's important that you realize that a no doesn't mean a bad deal. It just means a no for that particular party or that particular investor. And that's what my firm has become very good at, and we're actually very well known for it—is we know which group to take the specific loans to, to insure that people are going to get funding very quickly.

Then when borrowing this present money, there are a couple of nuances with it so, what should an individual be cautious of when borrowing private money?

You've got to be real cautious of the snakes and the sharks that are out there. And to avoid that in the greatest sense, or the easiest way possible, is do NOT sign on the bottom line until you have had confident attorney, or one that you trust and have a relationship with, do not sign anything until you have had them read every inch on that agreement on those forms.

Private money can be collateralized in such a way, that if you don't read the fine print, you might find yourself agreeing to put up assets or collateral that you didn't want to put up. You also may find yourself thinking that you agreed to a 36-month loan, but then when you read the fine print, it's only an 18-month loan.

If your exit strategy was created around the 36-month term, and 18 months into it you're getting called and they're threatening foreclosure on all of your assets and acquisition of your company, you can find yourself in a very, very tough spot very quickly. That's number 1.

Number 2, go in search of private money before the urgency in your situation increases, and let me illustrate that with an example.

We had a guy down in Phoenix, Arizona, who was buying a commercial property. He had had it under contract for several weeks, and he was looking for the funding on it, and he had several different sources that said they would put up the funding, but they kept pushing the funding back. "Oh we can do it next week—we can do it next week—we can do it next week."

His contract during that time is expiring. He keeps having to go back to the seller, the people that he's contracted with to buy it, to get extensions. Finally, the seller says, "We're not extending any more. You need to close next week or we're out of this deal."

Now he's found himself in such a tight financial position. He's allowed his earnest money to go hard, and if he doesn't close, he's going to lose $50,000, so the private money lender was now in a position that they could take advantage of the borrower.

Don't put yourself in a position where you have urgency, because the more urgency you have or need, the more you are going to pay for money. Give yourself plenty of time to go out and find these funding sources, and close early. And if you can't close early, then go out and find yourself a different lender.

Don't put yourself in a situation where your back is

against the wall, and you absolutely have to sign on that loan because it's the only option available to you. So be cautious of that. Those are really the two points that I would really encourage people to be aware of.

Okay, appreciate that. And let's change it up just a tad here because we've been talking about the client going out to get private money. What if one of our readers wants to be a private lender? How can I make money as a private lender?

How can you make money as a private lender? Am I assuming that you have your own money?

Yes.

Okay, so you have your own money, Nate. Tell me how much money we're dealing with.

We're dealing with $250,000.

Okay, so you're dealing in the $250,000 market and you're looking to place funds. Now if it's your money, first of all, I would encourage diversifying where you're putting your money out, and I would also diversify the length of time that you're putting your money out.

At $250,000, Nate, I would not encourage you to lend $250,000 in one opportunity or in one scenario. So if you find the guy who's got a half-million dollar apartment building that needs $250,000, I would not encourage you to lend on that. Mainly because if you put up all your liquidity in one project, if that project goes bad for whatever reason and you've got to foreclose to regain your investment or you've got to go through litigation to get your money back, your money is going to be tied up for a very long period of time.

Success of the private money lender is about diversification. Take the liquidity that you've got, and in your scenario, Nate, I would break it up into two or four different lending scenarios, so it might be the little small single family house where somebody needs to borrow 50 grand and their going to fix it up, clean it up, and flip it. "Great, here's 50 grand, pay me back in 90 days."

Then you find somebody else who needs to borrow $100,000, and you say, "Okay, great. I can give you $100,000 on that investment opportunity. Pay me back in six months."

Then you find somebody else who needs to borrow $150,000, and they only need it for short term, so you get it back in seven days.

We've got $50,000 in a three month deal, we've got $100,000 in a six month deal, and we've got $150,000 in a seven day deal.

In doing that, we're constantly rolling our money, and there's always a period of time where we're going to be getting our money back.

The first one's going to come back in seven days. We get it back, and we immediately put it into something else. And maybe we take the $150,000 and we split it into two

$75,000 deals.

But it's about diversification and minimalizing the risks. One of the easiest places to find opportunities to place funds is to just go down to the local foreclosure auction in your own town, or go down to your local tax sale. These sales happen almost every day across the country in some area and there are always people down there buying houses who need more funds.

I'll give you a personal example. I've got a guy right now who is going to be buying houses at auction, and he came to me and said, "Lee, I've got $100,000 to invest. What do you think I should do with it?" I said, "Well, you need to take your $100,000 and you need to leverage it with another investor who is willing to give you a 3-1 or a 4-1 leverage buy-down."

What that means is if I give you $100,000 as a private money lender, you will give me $300,000, or $400,000 in available funding.

So, Nate, for you if you've got your $250,000, you might go out and find an investor who has $100,000, and between the two now that's $350,000 that you could earmark for that guy to go buy houses at a foreclosure auction. Or it's $350,000 that could be leveraged to go invest in this opportunity, or that opportunity.

But the $100,000 that that investor is giving to you minimizes your risk and gives you a lower loan-to-value on the deals than you're going to find yourself involved in. So you can leverage it so that you're in the favored position, but always diversify.

Always have your money in multiple investments, paying off at multiple times. The worst thing you can do is take your $250,000 and put it into one investment and tell them to pay you back in a year.

Yes, so you want diversification is huge, and it keeps it safe for everybody as well.

Right.

And there are different ways of making money, obviously, with private money, whether you are lending it or borrowing it, but can I make money just brokering private money, even if I don't have any money of my own?

Absolutely. That's another thing I love about private money. As I mentioned private money doesn't discriminate as to the type of deals that it will go into. Nor does private money discriminate as to who it will communicate with.

There are people all over this country, and I don't claim to be real good at this, but there are people all over this country who are amazing networkers. They have this ability to go out and mingle and meet people, and talk to, and immediately develop rapport and trust with those individuals, but they may not have liquidity to be a lender themselves.

However, when you are one of those network people, you're not only identifying those who have funds and are sitting on millions of dollars of stocks, bonds, or retirement accounts. You are also identifying people and meeting with people who have a need for those funds. And you just merely put yourself in a position of the introducer.

So, Nate, you need to borrow $50,000, and I just happened to meet a guy at a cocktail party last night that's sitting on $100 grand that he'd like to put out, and I say, "Nate, I can help you find that $50,000," and I go to this other person over here, and I say, "Hey, I've got this guy that needs $50,000 that's on a property that's worth $150,000. It's a pretty low-risk scenario, but he's willing to pay 4 points and 13% interest on it. If you lend your $50,000 to Nate, would you mind paying me a couple of points?"

Well, what that means is if this guy lends you $50 grand, he's going to pay me $1,000 just for bringing him the opportunity. And that's what brokering is.

And the great part is, in most scenarios, and again, I'm not a licensed attorney in any state, so I would encourage you to seek legal counsel prior to doing this, but in most scenarios, licensing is not required to do this. So I don't have to go out and get a mortgage license to bring you two together and get paid a finder's fee.

That's why licenses aren't required for brokering in most scenarios is because we're not originating loans. We're merely getting paid for being a finder—a bird dog, if you will.

Okay. If you're going to broker those deals, or if

you're looking at your own deals with private money, how's the best way of going and evaluating these properties to make sure that it's a good investment?

Am I evaluating it as someone looking for money, or am I evaluating it as someone who's going to lend money?

You know, why don't we break down each scenario?

Okay.

Let's say you're looking at a piece of property to find money for.

Okay, if I'm looking for property to find money for, although there's certainly many different scenarios. The easiest scenario to get money for projects is an existing structure with an existing cash flow.

So again, going back to our $5 million apartment scenario, if we can tie that up for $5 million bucks and it has got $50,000 a month already coming in the form of cash flow. That is going to be the easiest opportunity to get lending on or for.

From there, second easiest opportunity is going to be a situation where you are getting it for a substantially reduced price, and these are going to be your cookie cutter deals. These are your neighborhoods where houses are selling for $50,000—nice cookie cutter little starter homes—first-time homebuyers things.

Every other house in the neighborhood is selling for $150,000, and you just happened to find the beat up, boarded up, dilapidated house, and you got it under contract for $60,000. That's a scenario where finding funding is going to be very, very easy for you to do.

I think the easiest way to explain it to people who are looking for a transaction that another investor would be interested in putting their money into is in this vernacular—think of it as your money. If you had the cash to do that type of scenario, to get into that opportunity, how much money would you be willing to put up on that project, on that opportunity? And people really need to stop and dissect what this means.

Especially with new investors, I see this a lot. They believe they have found the best deal ever, but they are not really seasoned at what makes a good deal, so they've identified a $100,000 house, and they've got it under contract for $85,000. Well, that's not a safe risk.

If it was $100,000 house and they had it under contract for $50,000, that'd be a great deal. So go out in search of these deals, thinking you are the one who's going to write the check. What type of deal would give you the comfort level that would make you willing to want to put up those funds?

So again 50-55 cents on the dollar is the sweet spot, if you can find deals in that price range. And this is as they sit, 55 cents on the dollar for what they are currently worth in their present condition. You cannot take into account after repair value and forced depreciation.

Most lenders look at the property for what it is right now because if I lend you money on a transaction where because you're claiming forced depreciation is going to reduce the loan's value scenario—sorry, if you don't show up on Saturday to put on a new coat of paint, put in new carpet, and spruce up the outside, it's only ever worth what it is right now.

So 55 cents on the dollar current value is the sweet spot. That's if you are looking to borrow funds.

Now if I'm a private money lender who's looking to put my own funds into a deal or broker funds for someone else, the scenario I'm looking for first before anything, is I'm looking for people who can put skin in the game. I want to lend to people that can put up to 15-25% of the amount they need for acquisition.

I want to see that they can put that up out of their own cash, or that they can use their own asset portfolio. And if they can't, then I want them to bring in someone else who can. For me as a lender, that's the sweet spot—someone who can put skin in the game. Preferably their own cash out of their own bank account.

That represents the safest investment for me because for them to depart and walk away from that opportunity and hand the keys back over to me, if they've got their own money in that, it's going to cause them a substantial amount of pain.

Let me give you an example. I've got a friend, who is doing a development, and he put up his personal residence for collateral for a $5 million loan, and he allowed this private money lender to attach a $1.8 million lien against his personal residence.

Well, this development went sideways 12-18 months ago, and I will tell you if he had not put up his personal residence as collateral on that loan, I'm guessing he probably would have already walked away by now, but because walking away means he's going to lose his house, he's going to do everything he can to salvage that investment and get that private money lender out of that loan.

And that's really what we look at as private money lenders; we want scenarios where it is as painful for you to walk away. So we're looking for that relationship loan.

That's amazing information. I wondered if you wanted to go in and evaluate the principal borrower's portfolio, and whether they are a safe risk for me and by borrowers. How would you go about that?

How would I go about looking at the principal borrower's portfolio?

Uh-huh.

The first thing I'm going to have them do is fill out a 1003, and the 1003 is the Universal Residential Lending form. It's created by HUD, and basically this form is 5-7 pages, and it's going to have them give me all their financial information, their list of assets, their list of liabilities, and it's going to give me a snapshot of their personal financial picture.

Now as confidential as that information and that data is going to be, it may or may not be 100% accurate, so even though good credit is not a requirement for getting private money loans, for me as a private money lender and a private money broker, I am going to require that I look at the buyer's credit report, because the credit report is a snapshot of what you have done in business up to this point.

Now the reason credit is not a requirement is this. When I look at your credit report, Nate, and I see that you've never purchased a car, you've never bought a house, never gotten financing for anything, even though you have pristine credit, let's say you have a credit score, but you have no credit history, I'm probably not going to loan to you because even though you have great credit, you don't have a history of succeeding in this particular investment opportunity.

Now if your credit report says that you've never borrowed money, but your financial statement says you've got this property, that property, and you've bought them all through seller financing and using creative financing strategies, I'm going to look at the two of those, and the one will trump the other because your 1003 and your financial statement, and your history, even though your credit is not telling me much, says you are a good investment risk.

Okay.

Now on the flip side of that, if you come to me, Nate,

and you've lost $10 million in the last market upheaval, I'm going to look at your financial statement and it might say that you owe nothing, but if I look at your credit report and I see that you've lost $10 million over the last 18 months, I'm still going to give you money.

Why? Because I see that you have an entrepreneurial spirit. You understand the game. You get it. And I'm sorry, but you do not make a substantial amount of money without taking on substantial risks. In this scenario now, obviously you were playing the game, and you were playing it well, and the market turned on you.

That happens, so I'm going to look at this and go, this guy knows what he's doing. Even though your credit sucks and you've got $10 million dollars of short-sales on your credit report, I'm still going to give you that loan because your credit tells me that you understand how to make money.

Yeah, you had some challenges, that happens, but you get it. So in that scenario, as much as credit is needed to get a snapshot of what you've been up to, your score is not going to be a consideration of whether or not your loan gets funded and that's whether I'm brokering that deal or whether I'm putting up my own cash on that deal.

Perfect. Now what would the remedy be if the private money borrower does not pay back the loan within the allotted time that the deal has been structured?

Again the short answer is foreclosure, either a foreclosure of the property or a seizure of the assets, depending on how the loan was collateralized in the first place. What people need to understand is when they are looking for private money, if they really want to break it down to the most elementary elements of investing, as a private money lender, when you come to me and say, "Hey, Lee, I want to borrow some money."

And I say, "Okay, great. What do you want to put up as collateral?"

And you say, "Here's the property address."

I'm going to go out and look at the property. And if I'm standing in front of that project or that house or that piece of raw ground, I'm going to be thinking to myself and I'm going to be looking at the amount of money you want to borrow and I'm going to be looking at that project, and the thing that is going through my mind is this, "Am I willing to own that project—that opportunity—that house, for this amount of money?"

And if my answer is yes, and I am willing to own it for this amount of money, then most likely you're going to get the loan.

But if you don't pay me back, my remedy now is to foreclose on you and regain possession of the real property, which is why it's so important that I would be interested in owning that opportunity.

So for me even though I grew upon a farm and I spent all of my summers throwing hay and bringing in crops, I'm not the guy to go to when you are a farmer in Ohio and you need to borrow $3 million to get you through the season on equipment. That's not my niche.

My niche is going to be cookie cutter development deals, single family homes, apartment building, where there is an existing cash flow. That's the type of opportunity I'm looking for. So to come to me and say "Hey, I want $3 million to bring my crops in," I'm not that guy. I don't have a tolerance for a risk in that niche, only because if the farm does not pay me back the $3 million bucks I don't want to go in and have to run his farm.

When I go out and look at that farm and go do I want to own all this production facility, all this land and all these cattle—do I want to own all that for $3 million, the answer is no. However, to a farmer that's been farming for years and years and years and gets it and knows that he could take that and make it a $10 million enterprise, then you're going to get the loan.

It's really about as a private lender, I'm willing to get involved in that risk for that reward or for that much money, I'm going to give you the loan but if you don't pay me back, I'm going to foreclose, I'm going to gain possession of the assets of the real property, and if there was any type of factoring involved in that collateral, whether it be inventory, or accounts receivable, I'm going to go in and seize those as well because that's my remedy because you didn't pay me back.

There are a lot of different ways to get financing in today's market. So as we're discussing private money,

what is the difference in private money and institutional loans?

The advantages of private money or institutional or conventional loans. First of all private money is faster. Private money is going to fund more quickly than conventional or institutional funds, especially if the amount of money that you're going to borrow is going to be funded 100% by one individual.

The reason it's faster it's one person who has to decide whether or not they're interested in the risk that you're putting up for the money that you're getting. When you go to conventional institutional places they have created boxes of requirements that you have to fit into if they're going to give you the money you're looking for, i.e. minimum credit score, minimum financial statement, minimum cash in the bank, and minimum years in the business.

If you don't meet every one of those line items then you're not going to get the loan. Institutional lenders are more interested in you, your past, your credit rating, your future, and less concerned in the opportunity itself. Because banks and institutional lenders are a niche, they are in the business of making loans and getting paid monthly. That's their model.

They have no desire to own real property, and they have no desire to take possession of your business, so if you don't meet every one of their criteria, you're not going to qualify. And banks and institutions usually only have one or two sources that they can go to get funding; whereas, a private lender or broker, they can go to literally millions of resources that I can take these opportunities to.

Point one, private money funds faster. Two, private money is less interested in you, more interested in the project, and three, private money can happen over a six-month period of time, a two-year period of time, a three-year period of time. Institutional conventional money is typically looking for ten, twenty, and thirty year notes where you may not need the money for that long of a period of time.

So we've talked about the advantage of private money, and that's great. I definitely think there is a huge difference between private money and conventional, but is there any scenario where you would use institutional or conventional as opposed to private money?

Yes. Scenario 1 is if you can get conventional or institutional money, you should, because typically it's going to be less expensive for you to get it and you're going to be able to get it for a longer period of time.

So if you're getting into an opportunity where you know you are going to portfolio that investment and you're going to run it for ten, twenty, thirty years, and you're going to hold on to it for a long period of time, conventional institutional money is going to be substantially cheaper, or more economical, than private money.

Conventional funds, let's say the farmer who wants to borrow $3 million, if he goes to a private money lender, the loans going to close very quickly, but he's probably going to pay from 4 to 8 points and he's going to pay anywhere from 12-18% interest on that loan. If he could qualify for a conventional loan, or a conventional line, he's looking for 1 or 2 points for origination and probably 7 or 8% interest.

Conventional money is certainly much, much less expensive. It's much more economical, but it's very slow and you've got to fit every one of the criteria to get the loan, but if you can get it, always go institutional, conventional, if you can get it. In today's economy though very few that need it can get it, and that's why private money right now is so huge.

With that said, actually, you know, conventional money is very, very tough right now, but with that said, how fast can the average person make money with this strategy?

Today. Literally, today, and I say that because this morning I got a call from a guy who needs to borrow $10,000. He's got some money in transition. He needs ten grand to get some things rolling in this business, and all he needs is $10,000 for a few days. He's got some money in transit. He's waiting for the money to hit, but he needs the funds to get something done today.

So if I can help this guy find $10,000 today, I can charge a brokering fee of $500 to a $1,000 bucks just for bringing together the guy who needs $10,000 with the guy who has $10,000. Now I'll tell you, for me, I'm probably just going to give the guy 10 grand because he's going to put up one of his investment properties.

It's a very low risk loan, but I can make $1,000 in just a few short days. So if I give him $1,000 on a $10,000 loan and 5 days from now he pays me back $11,000, I just made a $1,000 profit over a 5 day period of time. Now that's a 10% return on investment annually, but the fact that I did it in 5 days means it's about a 400% yield on my investment. That's a great loan.

Now whether I've got the 10 grand or not, I can just easily get on the phone and call my cousin or my uncle or my aunt or someone and say, "I've got this guy who needs 10 grand. Will you put it up? He'll give you $500 at the end of 5 days."

Well, if I told the guy to give me $1,000 and I told uncle that it's going to be $500, I'm going to make $500 just bringing the two of them together. It really, and I don't want to over-simplify it, but it really is easy. It really is easy, as long as you've got the opportunity. It really is easy.

I've been doing stuff with private money inside my business. I've learned some good stuff from you on some other strategies, but if someone wanted to learn more from you, what's the best place for them to go?

www.PrivateMoneyBank.com

Okay. That's www.PrivateMoneyBank.com, and if you were to have some final words for our readers, and recommendations, or words of wisdom for them to get rolling and get started with this strategy in leveraging this type of financing for their investment business,

what would it be?

Two things. First thing would be, go find a deal. Go find either an opportunity that you need funding for, or go find someone who has an opportunity that they need funding for.

Piece of advise number two would be to adopt my philosophy in life, which is this: In every social, economic, or business setting, it is my goal, my mission, to be the poorest, dumbest guy in the room, and I'm sure I could say that in a little more socially, friendly way. I want to be the poorest, dumbest guy in the room.

Because if I'm the poorest, dumbest guy in the room that means everyone in that setting can teach me something, or has more money than I do. And if I can find people to learn from and people that have money, I'm never going to have a hard time finding these individuals that I can take these opportunities to.

And so go out in search of these opportunities, and go out and find these people who have the funding to do these types of opportunities.

And from there educate. Get yourself engrossed in either real estate education, private money funding education.

I certainly provide those resources. You can get them at my web site, but there are also great books out there you can read and pick out and really become a student of this strategy because you can make a substantial amount of money doing this. As for me, I'm a college drop-out. I don't have a degree in high finance. So if I can do it, I truly believe that anybody can do it.

I didn't come into this business from the banking side. I actually got into this business from the investors side. Like many people, I got started by watching a late night infomercial and having this fast-talking guy tell me I could make millions of dollars buying and selling real estate. He was right. I went out and made millions of dollars buying and selling real estate.

The thing that bothered me more than anything though was the people that I was going to provide the funding for my deals were making as much, if not more than me, merely by putting up the funds and I was the guy out there doing all the work. I was the guy out there sweating to death, cutting my fingers with saws, and all kinds of things.

And I'm doing all this work, and the guys who are funding the deals for me are making just as much money while they are on the lake hanging out with their family on the weekend. And that really bothered me.

And I was going, "Wait a minute! Why are they any different than me?" Well, the answer was that they were not any different than me. The only difference was they knew this business and I didn't, and they knew where to go to find these funding sources and I didn't.

So I very quickly became a student of the finance world and where you can go to finance these types of loans. Who funds them? What bench markets are they looking for?

What represents a good investment opportunity?

And then just bringing those two people together, and sitting in the middle and making a pretty sizeable spread because of this knowledge. So if I can do it, anybody can do it. It's not difficult. It's not hard. You just need to educate yourself on these kinds of things.

Definitely. I really appreciate that and I'm sure that our readers do as well. Education is definitely key, so I know its one thing that I'm sure you continue to do for yourself. I know that I continue to do it on a day to day basis. Thank you so much for sharing some tips and strategies on private money. I know it's definitely going to benefit out readers and listeners about investing.

My pleasure. Thanks for having me. I've had a great time.

Thank you.

Chapter Four
Interview with Sean Carpenter

Alright, everyone. We're here today with a very special guest. His name is Sean Carpenter. I'll tell you what; he has some unbelievable knowledge and experience in the topic that we're going to be covering right now, which is Government Deal Funding.

Let me tell you a little bit about where he began. He started his career in real estate as an Acquisitions Officer for a national, Low Income Housing Tax Credits indicator, working on LIHTC transactions – don't worry, he may explain that a little bit more through the call for you, if you're wondering what that is – in the southeast and northeast regions of the United States.

He also has been an Asset Manager at Massachusetts Housing Finance Agency, where he maintained a portfolio of federally subsidized properties conducting annual inspections and regular financial and rent increase analysis, and participated in workout and recapitalization strategies.

Most recently, Sean has served as a Project Manager with a national development company, focusing on the preservation of expiring use of affordable housing. Sean also is on the staff of Senator Mark Montigny, working with constituents on a wide variety of public policy issues.

Sean is a graduate of the University of Massachusetts, Dartmouth, where he holds a Bachelor of Arts degree in Political Science. Additionally, he holds a Certificate of Real Estate Finance from Boston University.

Sean has unbelievable knowledge and experience. More importantly, he has community involvement, serving as a representative Town Meeting member and a Call Volunteer Firefighter, which is super important.

I think that, no matter what you do in life, whether it is in business or not, it's important to always be giving back. He's also a member of Sigma Tau Gamma fraternity, and currently resides in Quincy, Massachusetts.

What's really important here – I want you guys to understand the importance of what he's done – is that over the past 12 years, he's put together over a half a billion dollars – that's "billion" with a B, not an M – in deals using government programs.

He works with clients and students around the country to get tenants for their properties, with six- and seven-figure developer fees, millions in tax credits, and funding to cover rehab, down payments, and more. We're going to go into that real quick.

Sean, welcome. We're really happy that you're here to share this information with us.

Thanks, Nate. I know that's a lot there, but I'll tell you what: there's a great opportunity for everyone to participate in these programs.

Definitely.

It's an unbelievable thing with government funds, and so many people don't realize what is out there for funding.

Go Grab Your $247 of FREE Gifts at www.InsiderSecretsMoney.com

Some of these programs are 30 or 40 years old.

It's a great opportunity for folks who are building their real estate business, for folks who already have a real estate business, or for folks who want to change their real estate goals so that they can receive some funds.

I don't know how far you want me to go here, but I can tell you that, right now, I'm reading through a bill that's going through Congress that could put $48 billion on the street for real estate investors within the next six or eight months. That's what we're talking about here.

That's huge. With that said, Sean, why don't you tell us a little bit about what government funding is, so we can get a good understanding?

Government funding is actually the very simple term that I coined to make people understand that the government has a ton of programs out there to supplement folks' real estate activities.

It comprises a number of different avenues, and I break it down into, basically, four parts. You have hard financing, which is just regular financing that's backed by the government: FHA and bond programs that are out there that are available.

Then you have soft loan programs, which look like grants, but they're not, zero percent loans, forgivable loans, and things like that. Then there are tax credits, which you can sell for profit to build your real estate for various activities.

Then, the last piece is the government funding that comes in the form of operational subsidies. Many people know about Section 8 and things like that. All of the different funds will fall into one of those four categories. At least, that's how I make it easy for my students to learn it.

Okay. Have you done quite a few deals using the government funding?

As you've said earlier, I've done over $500 million worth of transactions, everywhere from Low Income Housing Tax Credit transactions to Historic Tax Credit transactions and conventionally financed FHA multi-family deals. I've even done bond deals. I've done complicated bond transactions, and then not-so-complicated bond transactions that spin off a lot of money.

Earlier, when introducing me, you talked about my experience with expiring use Section 8 projects. That's a huge, huge, huge thing right now, going through the real estate for the commercial markets.

Those are basically low-hanging fruit: properties that are for sale that don't have a big "For Sale" sign outside of them, finding those expiring use projects.

Those are projects that actually had subsidies on them for years, and the owners are deciding as their term of affordability – or whatever the restrictions were when they received the government fund – is ending. Those properties are pretty much being sold.

What we do here, just in my own consulting firm and

Development Company, is go out and buy those properties. We buy them for next to nothing because most of those people are just looking to get out. They've made their money, and they're ready to go. That's a lot of the stuff that we're doing these days.

That's called "preservation": preserving the affordability of these government-funded projects. By doing that, we actually automatically qualify for additional programs that are out there, like tax credits, home funding, and things like that.

Hopefully, we'll be able to break down even more in depth some of these government funding sites, too. Who is this available to? Our main readerships here are investors. Outside of that, though, and maybe even with investors – maybe we can focus on that – who is using the government funds?

Let me just give you an example about who qualifies, because that's a great question. Who qualifies for the funds? I don't know anybody who doesn't qualify for the funds, unless it's somebody who's not from the U.S. Essentially, this is money that's funded by taxpayers, and everyone qualifies to receive it.

However, the fact is that most of these funds don't go to individuals. They go to corporations, but for real estate related activity. As long as you've got a plan, an idea, and a project going, you would qualify for these funds. That said, who's getting it right now? Right now, there are a lot of big developers out there that are receiving these funds.

Go Grab Your $247 of FREE Gifts at www.InsiderSecretsMoney.com

I always use a joke when I'm talking to people. Think about those big developers sitting out there. They've just put up another project, and they've got their funds. They're sitting in the conference room, smoking their cigars and drinking their cognac. Everybody wants to be in that conference room.

Well, I've been in that conference room. I've been with those guys. I'm talking about guys who have gone from bankruptcy court to doing deals off the back of their yachts. It's amazing where people can start.

I have a friend who is also a student and a client of mine. He started with a six-family building. Now he's done another six-family, and he's now looking at 30-, 40-, and 50-unit buildings. He's really ramping it up. I also know other developers that are starting with 4000-unit portfolios. It's just a matter of where folks are comfortable.

In using those funds, now, are they going to have to come out of pocket – their own money – or are these fully funded by government funds?

I'm not a big fan of the no-money-down scenario. I know a lot of folks say, "No money down."

Have I done deals where no money down is possible? Yes. In fact, right now I'm doing a deal and I'm taking very little money out of my pocket.

However, that's not always the case. People have to be very, very cognizant of the fact that, with no money down, if it sounds too good to be true, it most likely is. It's all about deal structuring. This is a very simple thing.

If you have money in your pocket, you may have to use it. If you don't, you may have to find other ways to get it, and I can show people how to do that through pre-development funding, seed money, or low-interest capital for small businesses and things like that.

Essentially, a lot of these programs are coupled with other programs. For instance, if you're going to get a home loan for a 20-unit property, that's only going to cover about 20% of your costs or less. The rest of it has to be taken with a conventional loan.

However, if you think about it for commercial projects, you're getting about 70% loan to value. So, if you're adding in another 20%, that's a great rate, so you only have 10% out of your pocket. Hopefully, that makes sense.

Definitely. You mentioned a bill that they're talking about now. How much money are we actually talking about here? How much has the government set aside for people to leverage for these properties?

I can't even tell you the total number. I've often thought, "Maybe I should spend half a day and actually figure out how much money is dished out every year." I could probably do that, but I know that it's in the billions of dollars a year. The tax credit programs alone exceed $50 billion.

Let's take a step back for the Stimulus Bill. A new program was created in the Stimulus, and four and a half billion dollars were actually released for housing activities.

That one's called the Neighborhood Stabilization Program.

That was actually a program that existed from the year before, when they had the Foreclosure Bill. That was another four and a half billion dollars that was released for the Neighborhood Stabilization Program. Essentially, now, you have nine billion dollars, just in one program, that was released to all the states.

Let me just take a second and explain to you how this works. These programs are generally federally funded that get dished out to the states and some of the larger cities. What happens is that it trickles down through that funnel to Main Street.

If you're in state or a larger city, particularly a city with more than 50,000 people in it, you would go to your local agency. If you're in a smaller city, you might go to the State. So, there are state programs and local programs. Generally, though, it's all federally funded.

So, there's definitely a lot opportunity, then, that's out there. We're talking about billions of dollars. I guess that leads me into my next question, then.

If you watch the news, it's always horrible, horrible, horrible. Realistically, though, for investors, my belief is that it's a great time. What's your belief on that, given the current market conditions? Is it a good time for investors to be investing in real estate?

Yeah. There's never been a better time than right now. I tell this to folks all the time. I say it time and time again to folks when I travel around the country talking about this. I even say it to my staff: "Guys, we've got to get out there, getting these funds."

The government is continuously pumping money into real estate because real estate drives the economy. We haven't even seen yet the commercial fallout. We've seen the residential foreclosures, but the commercial markets tend to lag behind for a little while.

We haven't even started to see the commercial foreclosures that are happening. Yes, they're upticking a little bit now, but in the next six months, you're going to start seeing huge commercial fallout.

That means that the government – like they've bailed out the car industry and like they've bailed out the banking industry and the insurance industry – is going to have to bail out the commercial real estate markets. That's really the market that I hang around in.

Is there a time? If there's somebody right now who's listening to this call or reading this, who is thinking about whether or not it's a good time to be in real estate, they shouldn't be thinking about it anymore. It's just time to jump in.

I had a guy come into my office the other day. He's got a four-unit building and he said, "I want to get some funds for this."

I said, "Will you stop thinking about four-unit buildings, and start thing about 40-unit buildings, please?

People think that because you have four units, it's easy to manage. There's no difference between managing four units and 40 units. It's just a numbers game.

Yes, though; the opportunities are endless out there right now. For folks who understand what's going on and are getting that specialized knowledge of getting into these funds, it's a very, very, very good time to be in there.

If I can tell you for one second, I just was talking to somebody in a state. I won't mention what state this is because it's not public yet. They have hundreds of millions of dollars that they have to get rid of by the end of the year because not enough people were taking advantage of these funds.

That's huge. I'm sure there are probably some other states out there that need to do that, as well.

Yeah, and that's just one state. The only reason I knew that is because I was out at an event. There just happened to be a bunch of practitioners, and I was talking to somebody in this one state agency. It's just amazing.

This was a smaller state, too. God only knows what the larger states have for funding, that have to be dished out by the end of this year. This is happening all the time because the government doesn't advertise these programs.

I joke about the Super Bowl. They had a Super Bowl ad for the census. People were saying, "I can't believe we spent this much money."

Wouldn't it be amazing if they actually started advertising some of these funds that they have available? Some of these programs are 30 years old. People would start using them, wouldn't they?

Oh, yeah, for sure. That's what we're doing here: trying to educate. That's why I'm excited about you being a part of this and being able to educate people on these alternative sources that are available to them. Just because conventional may be tough for an investor these days, does not mean that there isn't money available.

With that said, I've got a question, here, that I'm thinking of. A lot of times, people are probably saying, "Oh, man. I don't want to deal with the government. I'm sure there are all kinds of red tape I've got to go through."

How long does it usually take to line up some funds, depending on the deals you're doing through government funding?

I did a $22-million transaction in just over 60 days.

Twenty-two million in 60 days? Wouldn't you think that would take about a year to line up?

Yeah, some of them do. I have to be honest here. Everybody's saying, "I want to close in 30 days." If folks are ready to close, then you can close in 30 days. It's not a whole lot different than the conventional markets.

People get all crazy about these applications and

everything else. Have you ever seen an application for a commercial mortgage from a regular bank? It's no different than what you'd see to get funding from a government agency.

The reality is this. Why does everybody think that it's tough to get these applications in? Why do you think that that happens? I'm going to tell you why that is.

Who's telling everybody that the applications are horrible? The people who've already received the funds. What incentive would those people have to tell you that the application process is just not worth it? The incentive is that they get all the money to themselves. That's the reality.

These are my clients that are out there. I have a business of just filling out applications for people. I don't do it myself, but we have folks here who do it. It's not a difficult process.

Those clients of mine that have been doing this for years and years and years and for whom I fill out the applications, are not happy that I'm out, going around the country and teaching people about these funds.

The government loves me, by the way. You'd think that they'd get mad that I was out there trying to teach people, but the government loves it. I'm actually helping people get the specialized knowledge that they need to go forward and get these applications in quickly, so that they're done correctly.

Not only that, but these students out there who are

learning this stuff can then become consultants. If you don't want to do your own deal, you can become a consultant and teach other people this information. Or you can advise cities and towns that don't have the staff, and you can help them get the applications processed.

The opportunities are endless. It doesn't have to be your own deal. If you're not ready to pull the trigger, you can do somebody else's deal and still get paid a fee for it. That's really how easy it is.

We did this deal. It's 85 units. I'll call it a five-million-dollar deal. We started in January, and we closed in March. It was just an FHA multi-family finance deal. My consulting fee on that was $45,000, and that's allowable. That's allowable because somebody has to fill out the application.

Now, let me tell you a little secret about that application. It was very simple, and we only did it once. You hear about people who have to do it time in and time out. You don't have to do that. A lot of this stuff is automated now. It's all on the computer. It's very easy.

We, obviously, are happy when people want us to do it for them. It's really funny that people think that the application process is tough, but that's all I'll say.

I think you hit the nail on the head there with that. There are people who have access to money and know where to get it, and they don't want everyone else coming in to get it.

I'm just thinking about one thing that I've taken

Go Grab Your $247 of FREE Gifts at www.InsiderSecretsMoney.com

away from what you just said: **$45,000 within a three-month time frame is $15,000 a month. More importantly, it's just another revenue stream inside your business. You don't even have to be doing real estate deals with government funding to make money. I think that's huge.**

Yeah. I use that as an example because a lot of times, folks are very concerned about taking the risk on their own. When you show them how they can actually help another developer get a deal done and get paid for it by the government – it's all part of the funds that you get – it's amazing.

There are obviously a lot of different types of deals. Can you explain a little bit about the different types of deals that you can leverage with government funding?

Sure. I do tend to talk a lot about multi-family commercial properties. I can't even tell you the different types of projects that are out there. I've worked on a YMCA. I've worked on charter schools. I've obviously worked with multi-family housing.

We just had somebody come in with a private airport that they're looking at. I've worked on a lobster pond. I've worked on commercial office buildings. I've worked on industrial buildings and vacant lands. I'm actually doing one here myself. It's a piece of vacant land and it's on the Cape Cod Canal.

There's just so much more. Folks don't realize that any project at any time may qualify for these funds.

Go Grab Your $247 of FREE Gifts at www.InsiderSecretsMoney.com

What about residential properties?

That's the toughest thing to show people. I know there are a lot of people who are flipping houses, and they're doing wholesaling, short sales, and all that stuff.

I'm no different, actually. I dabble in that every once in a while, particularly when I need some drinking money. I'll go out and flip a house. There's nothing like going to the bar with $25,000 in your pocket.

However, the reality is that single-family flipping is a profit center, and I think the government recognizes that. Are there opportunities to do it? Yes, there are newer opportunities every day because of the growing foreclosure prices.

Neighborhood Stabilization Program was designed to get public funding into cleaning up the foreclosure mess in barrios and things like that. Funds are being used from the government at zero percent. Forty-year loans are being used to help developers buy and rehab and sell single-family residential. That's not as common as the other programs that are available everywhere, but those are opportunities.

Just let me say for a second that for folks who are buying single-family residential and want to rent it, the operating subsidies are always there. Section 8 and things like that are always available to help out get rents up and things like that.

So, the potential is not when you're flipping properties. It doesn't make sense to flip properties with the

government funding. Is that what you're saying?

Yeah. Think about what flipping is. Flipping is essentially buying low and selling high, right?

Exactly.

The reason why the government pumps money into any given industry is because they're trying to get it to go. They're trying to give it leverage and keep it going. There's no need to infuse money into an industry like single-family flipping. It's already a profitable industry, so there's really no need to infuse capital into that.

Again, for the developers who are doing it in large amounts, yes, there are funds available. You can convince the government to pretty much do anything, as long as you have an argument. Sometimes it's just a matter of going and picking up the phone, calling somebody, and saying, "This is my idea. Can I get a little assistance for it?"

With that, obviously there is a wide range of properties in regards to what you can use government funding for, but is there a wide range or different types of government programs available?

Oh, yeah. As I was saying earlier, you have the hard financing programs, the soft financing programs, and the tax credit program. Just let me give you an example of tax credits, because that's where folks ask, "What does that even mean?" and they shy away from that.

Number one, it's probably some of the most profitable

areas of the industry. Number two, it's a huge opportunity and has developed more units nationwide than probably any other program.

Just taking tax credits, we have Low Income Housing Tax Credits and State Low Income Housing Tax Credits. Then you have Historic Tax Credits that are federal and state Historic Tax Credits; New Market Tax Credits, and Renewable Energy Tax Credits. Then, in the individual states, you might have Solar Tax Credits or different types of tax credits. That's on the commercial sector.

We've all heard about the Homeowner Tax Credit. For instance, if somebody wants to just buy their first house, they get an $8,000 tax credit. That doesn't have to be a single-family. It could be a one- to three-family, so that is an opportunity for somebody, as well.

Plus, there are renewable energy upgrades for your own house if you want to do windows, insulation, or things like that. So, yes, there are a lot of different programs out there. Some are big and some are small.

You're talking about the tax credits, and you mentioned the difference for each program. How does that actually work?

The tax credits essentially go like this. For the commercial tax credits, if you have a project, you get allocated tax credits, either competitively or through a formula. You take those credits, and you sell them off to institutional investors, who then become investors in your project.

Just to take a side note here, there are a lot of folks who are probably reading this right now, saying, "Isn't that what private syndication and private money is?"

Yes, but you're trying to raise private capital for your project. Imagine if you actually had something to give them right away, like a tax credit.

Essentially, that's what we do. We sell those tax credits off to banks and insurance companies and, in some cases, individuals; and we use the funding for that to develop the project.

That said those investors who buy those credits get those credits over a ten-year period for the Low Income Housing Tax Credit. For the Historic Credit it's five years, and for the New Market it's seven years.

This is so much good information that you're bringing here. I really appreciate that. Beyond just the funding, I'm sure the government can help otherwise. Is there anything that they can do to help? Also, can they get you tenants, as well?

Yeah. One of the things that folks do all the time when they think about government funding for projects is think about it as Section 8. Section 8 has a really negative connotation.

I worked in the Section 8 program for five years, and it's a very good program. It helps a lot of folks get off their feet. Also, though, it's a great program for those investors out there who have vacant units in their properties. They need to get a normal, consistent rent stream and get paid on the first of every month. That's essentially what we're talking about.

Imagine what it would be like to have those rents direct deposited into your bank account on the first of every month from the government, instead of having to chase tenants around. They still have a portion to pay, but you don't have to go chasing around the government to get the money. They just deposit it in your account the first of every month.

That's just one program; the Section 8 program. There's also a program called VASH, which is becoming more and more popular, because it's housing homeless veterans around the country.

There are hundreds of thousands homeless veterans around the country, and this program is actually there to assist those homeless veterans and to get them off the street and into housing.

For those of you who are thinking, "I do have ten vacant units on my property," you might want to pick up the phone and call the VA.

So, it's more vast than just the funding side. They can not only help you get the money for the deals you want to do, but also help you with the people with the deals to make that a profitable cash-flowing piece.

Absolutely. That becomes more and more difficult when you get out of the residential and you get more into the commercial side, but there are a lot of different programs that are out there. There are so many different needs out there that different programs can be morphed into your projects. One thing people always say is that the laws are always so ambiguous. You've got to use that to your advantage.

Definitely. In your opinion, how do you think the Foreclosure Bill affects us investors?

The Foreclosure Bill – and I call it "The Conception of Stimulus" – was in 2008. That Foreclosure Bill was when the residential foreclosure crash was really getting ramped up.

I don't know if folks can remember back that far, but this was really when we started seeing huge foreclosures just rising up. There were thousands and thousands of foreclosures that were happening all over the country.

The government quickly – and I use that term lightly, because Congress moves very slowly – moved to get this Foreclosure Bill passed, and get a ton of money out on the street. It was four and a half billion dollars, just for investors, through the Neighborhood Stabilization Program, to buy up foreclosed properties and get them back onto the rolls.

A lot of these properties were abandoned. People left them – three families or four families; it doesn't matter – and these funds were used to help get those properties rehabbed.

There are a number of states that still haven't even used

those funds. To make things worse – or better, depending on how you look at it – in the Stimulus Bill, which happened a couple of months later in February 2009, they added another four and a half billion dollars to that program.

So, investors, go get your piece of the pie. Go get your Stimulus money. That is available in all the major cities around the country. Every single state received allocation.

As you said, it depends on how you look at it. It could be a huge opportunity. You've got a wealth of knowledge on this topic. Just looking at your experience, as we talked about when you first came on, you've got a lot of pieces in there.

Let's switch the mode here a little bit. How would someone go about finding these types of government funds or even the properties that qualify for the government funds to see if they could maybe leverage some marketing in their business? What would be a way that they could do that?

Selfishly, I would say that they would call me, but this is supposed to help people get their business off the ground. Locally, folks can go down and check it out through different agencies.

This is the way that I really put this stuff out. There's a three-step process that I really use to try to explain. It's called Pick the Program, Submit the Application, which we talked about, and Use the Funding.

The thing here is that a lot of people get really excited about these programs and these opportunities. Then they just go into an agency and say, "I have this project and I need it funded. What do you have?"

People who do that are not very successful. However, if people know the exact program that they want – for instance, if they want Low Income Housing Tax Credit – then they go and they look that up in the agency that's there. We have a Web site that actually spells that out for folks.

They can go, and the application will be there for them. They can fill it out, talk to the appropriate agency staff, and get that funded quickly. That's the way that we often do it.

These funds are available in so many different avenues that, literally, people are walking by the funds on their way to a closing in that format. They're just everywhere.

It may be as simple as going to a local economic development agency. It might be going to a state housing agency. It may be going to HUD. It just depends on the program.

Maybe you won't mind sharing with us one of your more successful deals that you've done using government funding. Would you share that with everyone?

I have so many deals that I've done. I like to use this example. This was another 85-unit building. This was that $22-million project I talked about. We closed it in just over 75 days.

I like to say that we pimped up Grandma's house. Grandma's not sitting over in the corner licking the lead paint chips off the windowsills anymore. We really gave

Go Grab Your $247 of FREE Gifts at www.InsiderSecretsMoney.com

her new luxury housing to live in.

This was an elderly building in Boston with 85 units. We redid the kitchens and the bathrooms. When we redid the bathrooms, we took out the bathtubs and we put in stand-up showers to make it easier for these folks to get in and out of the showers, because it's an elderly complex.

It was 100% Section 8, [36:15 but property-based Section 8]. So, the Section 8 doesn't stay with the tenant; it actually stays with the building. We generated about six and a half million dollars worth of tax credits, and we sold those off for $6.2 million.

The developer on that deal – and I was a consultant on that deal, and I'm on the Board of that building, as well – was a non-profit developer that received a Developer Fee of $1.2 million.

The non-profit Board that I'm a part of received another fee of $200,000; and we did everything there. We did the elevators. We put in new community rooms. We put in a new lobby and redid the units. It was just a fantastic project and a great way for these folks who were living there.

Their average age is 79 years old for all those 85 units. Now they're living in beautiful apartments in downtown Boston. That's probably the most successful, and the one that I'm most proud of.

However, I've done deals much larger than that. I've done $30 million and $40 million deals where we've done the same thing.

You mentioned a non-profit that did those deals. Do you have to be a non-profit organization to get government funding, or can you be a for-profit organization?

Actually, it's funny. Whenever I mention non-profits, a lot of folks think that you need to have a non-profit to get a lot of these funds. The answer is "No." You don't need to be a non-profit. It just so happens I work with a lot of non-profits.

A lot of for-profit developers out there are receiving government funds. A good national name is Archstone or Avalon Communities. These are folks that are receiving government funds all the time. Big developers like Equity and like that are receiving huge amounts of money, and those are all for-profit companies.

Non-profits tend to be favored more. I have a non-profit foundation that we use because they become part owners of our projects. We score better on our applications to have a non-profit piece.

It's not that I just have a sitting non-profit there. This is a non-profit that actually does and has a mission. They carry out their mission day in and day out with resident services, social services, and things like that.

You don't just create a non-profit to have it sit on the sidelines, just so you can get better on your applications. You actually have to do what you say you're going to do, essentially. However, non-profit participation is not a requirement.

Here's just a curious question I have. When you set up a non-profit piece, does it have to be geared towards the type of funding you're going towards, or can you have your non-profit mission statement say "Help young, inner-city entrepreneurs," or stuff like that; but it's not actually geared towards maybe providing housing for people?

Does it matter what that non-profit does? Obviously, it needs to be something beneficial, but does it have to be in line, exactly, for the funding you're going with?

That's a great question. I get asked that a lot. I'm not an expert on developing non-profits, that's for sure. However, I can tell you and I can advise folks that a very good way to create a non-profit for your real estate business is to keep it as generic as possible.

I sit on the Boards of four non-profits. For instance, one of the non-profits is a school; so, obviously, their mission is school based. For the others, though, it's real estate, so we drive it towards affordable housing, helping low-income communities, and community development.

There are certain forms you have to fill out when you say things like "community development," so that's just another thing out there. Yes, though, you have to identify what it is that you're doing.

That makes sense. That answers that question. I appreciate it. I don't want to overwhelm everyone, but you've got just so many moving pieces, which is great.

You definitely shed some light on this for investors, letting them know that there are available funds for us as investors in today's economy. There are ways to get access to them. The key is that if you can understand it, you can get it.

You have a wealth of knowledge on this topic beyond just doing your own deals. I already get the impression, as you mentioned, that you do help others do deals; but in what way do you help others get funding for their deals?

Personally, the ways that I help folks is that, for newer investors, we may partner up with our students to help them get that first deal off the ground.

Sometimes, we come in as a consultant, and we advise folks on how to structure their deal and what funds to go after. We also help folks just by educating them on the sources of funds that are available, and by doing things like this.

If one person who's reading this right now goes out and does a deal because they learned about a program that they didn't know about, it's a success.

That's one of the things that we're constantly doing; educating the public about the funds that are available, but also walking them through and getting their deals funded.

So, pretty much A to Z, you're there to help people, whether they need you on a consulting level or whether they need you to be in the deal with them from A to Z to

get it done. You're there pretty much every step of the way if they need it.

Yeah. Unfortunately, a lot of that just eats into our time. We help a lot of people get a lot of deals. Before I got smart about my business, I used to do it for free. Imagine that.

No, I would not expect you to do anything for free. You have some very, very useful knowledge that people should be paying for, no matter what.

With that said, if someone does leverage government funding, do they have to stay local with it? You touched on this earlier. I've not done government funding, which is why I was so intrigued to be able to get on the phone with you and learn about this.

Let's say I lived in Georgia and I wanted to do deals in North Carolina through that. Am I able to do that, or is it more of a localized-style program?

That is a fantastic question. I get asked that a lot. I can tell you that while we're having this conversation, I'm sitting in my office in Quincy, Massachusetts, looking out the window. It's a sunny day, just for the record, which is rare.

Right now, as I sit here talking to you, we are closing on a project in Phoenix, Arizona. As I talk to you, I'm underwriting deals in Indianapolis, in Florida, and all over the country. Most of the deals that I've done have not been in Massachusetts.

I was born and raised in Massachusetts, as you can

probably tell from my funny accent. I've lived here my whole life, but I've done deals in Mississippi, Alabama, Arkansas, Tennessee, and then right up through the New York-New Jersey area, and as far west as California.

I think that's great for everyone to know. Sometimes people do invest across, and they run across deals through other areas. It opens up their backyard to wherever they want it to be at that point, so that's great.

For everyone who's reading right now, if they wanted to learn more about getting government funding, working with you, or hiring you as a consultant, what do they need to do in regard to getting funding or getting a hold of you to get some more information?

We typically only work with our students. If folks want to work with us directly, there's a significant retainer, but if they want to become our students, they can come onto the Web site and become one of our students. We actually offer free consulting to get them off the ground. Then, obviously, going forward the more that they need, we charge for that.

Folks can start working with us, though, coming in as students. Our Web site is **www.GetPublicFunding.com**. That's how folks can get in touch with us.

Now, here's the deal. There's one piece that we didn't talk about, and I want to bring this in because it's important as we start to talk about how to get these deals funded, how to get this done quickly, and how to work with us.

There's one other piece to the puzzle. There are a lot of consultants out there, who are doing this, but they miss this one piece of the puzzle, and it's something we focus on every single day. As I'm having this conversation with you, I just came from a meeting on this very subject.

It's politics. I know people cringe when they see that word or hear that word said. I know that, but here's the deal. Politics is a huge component to your real estate business.

Government funds or not, you need public support for your projects, and that's another whole piece that we teach. We show people how to contact your Congressman and how to contact your local officials to get public support for your project, because it opens up another whole avenue.

Because I'm politically active – and I've been a political consultant for a number of years – not only do I get funds for my projects, but I also get leads on projects that are happening, as well. That's a whole other piece that our students get that many other consultants around the country do not provide. Programs, particularly, those that have books and tapes and are selling home study courses, don't teach this component.

I don't care if you're doing single-family flipping or a commercial project with me, that political piece is so very important. That's something that we take very seriously, and we've been so successful at it.

That's a unique skill set to have. You have that and you've worked close with it. We started out the call talk-

ing about your experience. What better person to learn how to do that from yourself?

If I go on a rant about healthcare policy, though, you probably don't want to be around me on that!

Well, let's leave that. That could be a two-hour call, if not longer.

If you could give one word of advice or one action plan to our readers, what would you tell them to do first in regard to getting more information, to getting started, or deciding whether or not this is for them?

The first thing I would tell people is to stop sitting on the sidelines. I was involved in a charter school movement with an Asian community locally, here, in Boston. They asked a very similar question: "What can we do to help our prospects better?"

In that case, I said, "Do you know what you can do as a community? You can start to vote."

That doesn't translate well to the real estate community, but here's what I find when I go to REIA meetings and different networking groups around the country. I wouldn't call myself a master networker, but I do enjoy the free coffee and sodas at meetings all over the country.

People ask me all the time, "How do we get going?"

You get going by stop talking about the deals and start doing the deals. Instead of looking for that deal that hasn't come down the line, take the deals that are in front of you.

I think what happens is that people have to get focused on what looks like a great opportunity.

One of the things that I often hear is five "No's," before I hear a "Yes." When we write our prospects out – we write a deal summary on every deal that comes through our door – we put pros and cons either for an offering memorandum or just for a perspective that we're going to send to a government agency. I often tell folks, "For every negative, I want two positives; and you have to have a negative."

When folks are looking to get started on that first deal, I want you to go and make a list of everything that's bad about the project. If you list off 10 things, I want you to list off 20 positive things. Just by doing that alone, you convince yourself that this deal is good. If you can't come up with the 20 things, then maybe it's not the right deal for you.

I think what happens so often, though, is that folks just talk and talk and talk about the deals, and they never take action. It's time to take action.

For the folks who are investing in real estate, when the crash in 1989 happened, when the crash in the late 1990s happened, and the one in the early 2000s, the people who made the most money were the people who learned about the programs that were available, they realized the potential, they took action, and they took risks. You're not going to get any reward without risk. Now those people are sitting here and saying, "What recession?"

That's a huge golden nugget and some great advice, for sure. I hope everyone understands that that is the biggest thing. Get off the sidelines, get access, and learn what's available to you.

I agree with you. What recession? If you have everything in place, there isn't one.

Right.

Sean, I really appreciate your time, sharing this information with our readers. I know they've learned from it and I know they're going to want information.

Definitely, do forget to go to www.GetPublicFunding.com and check out more information. If you feel like government funding is for you and you want to start tapping into the unbelievable amount of resources that are available to you, definitely do that.

From what I've learned about him and know about him, and also from talking to him here, I believe Sean is one of the leading experts in this style business and getting this kind of money. He talks the talk and he walks the walk. He does it all.

Sean thanks so much for providing so much amazing content and information to our readers.

Thanks, Nate. That's so true about walking the walk. We hear about people all the time who are out there who are teaching you how to buy this or that, yet they've never done it themselves.

I can honestly tell you that this is stuff that I've been working on for the last 12 to 15 years, depending on what type of project it is. This is what I've been doing for my whole career.

You're not going to find too many folks out there. I know I'm singing my own praises right now, but I just want people to understand why certain things are important.

There are three sides of every deal. There's the investment side, there's the regulatory side, and then there's always the developer's side. I've worked on all three sides of those deals. Just a little bonus section: I've also worked in politics. It's a good component.

So, whether you work with me or not is not an issue. What I'm telling is that, when you're looking for folks who are going to work with you, make sure that they have all the components to bring to the table to make you successful. I want you to be successful. There's plenty of money to go around, and I'm not going to keep it all for myself.

Thanks, Nate, for having me.

I appreciate it, Sean.

Chapter Five
Interview with Melanie Ansel

All right. So today we are on a call with Melanie, and which I'm actually very, very excited about is what we're going to be talking about is how to become bankable. Which I think is very, very important for investors these days and just a little background about Melanie. She has over 30 years of experience in commercial lending and banking management, and Melanie has spent her entire banking career assisting small businesses through lending, coaching and training, and she's held the position of regional president with First Commonwealth Bank overseeing the business development for six county market and with an extensive experience in commercial lending. Melanie provides expertise in loan structuring and lending solutions to her clients. Through her involvement with a family owned business, Melanie has learned to analyze the business requests from both sides. Of the banker's desk lending with compassion and a true understanding of the many stages of small business ownership. So as an instructor Melanie educates the young entrepreneur to the seasoned business owner on proper business planning, on what to expect during the loan process, and the challenges of being self-employed. So Melanie I'd like to welcome you to the call.

Thank you.

All right, well let's go ahead and let's get into the meat and potatoes of what we can uncover for people today and what does My Business Builders do?

My Business Builders has numerous components. We help people that want to go into business. We help people that are all ready in business and possibly need a little update of their or diversification of their product line. They need to identify a niche. They need to understand cash flow. They need to improve the bottom line. We also help real estate investors on again how to become bankable, how to prepare a package for a bank and we basically do the shopping for all of our clients. Being that I'm connected in the banking world and have been involved in banking so long I know people at every banking institution that is out there, and I can place the client with the correct banker so their credit score only gets hit one time.

Right now a lot of people are going to numerous banks and the very first thing a banker does is pull your credit. Obviously the credit scores going to drop. Then that banker says, "Oops you don't meet our minimum score" which I have seen over the last couple of months that minimum scores are now 700. So a person goes to a bank, doesn't meet the minimum score requirement, just had their credit score drop, and then they move onto another. What I do is help that client package their request. I find them the bank that I know is going to approve them or if they're not approvable then I can put them through classes. I can do one-on-one coaching, whatever is needed to get them to the point that we're forming a plan of action to get them to bankable. Some of my students it takes a couple of months, some of my students it takes a year depending on how bad the credit is, what the cash flow looks like, if there's consolidations needed. So we look at the personal end of their business, plus the business end of the business.

Okay, and you know I definitely think that's a great little niche for investors and business owners because a lot of times they are constantly flapping in the wind almost in regards to just trying to get lending, and I think you mentioned the thing where they go from one bank to the next bank, to the next bank and it really deters them and gets them frustrated.

Exactly.

Being able to deal with just you, I think is absolutely amazing and someone they don't have to worry about, they can add you to their team. You know.

Exactly.

So I think that's great. Now and one question I know, I'm sure you hear this question all the time, and but I do as well, and people always want to know are banks lending money?

The answer is yes and no. You have to go in prepared. Before you sign a sales agreement I cannot emphasize enough that they have to make sure that they, their idea, their real estate, whatever it is that they're doing is bankable; how to do that again we teach them that, how to prepare that package. Everyone of my clients that have prepared a package, whenever I present it to the bank because I'm actually the one that meets with the bank or shows them the package and says, "Okay, do you think you can approve this?" every single one of those bankers has said, "Wow" when they see the package. So if you go in prepared, yes you're bankable. If you don't go in prepared odds are they're just going to run your credit, if you don't have that magical credit score that they want, you're probably going to be turned down, when literally if you present yourself right even if your credit score is a little bit lower, you normally can get approved.

The other thing is you have to find a banker that is educated. In today's banking world and as big as banks have gotten, there always the local branch is not the place to go. Some banks have business lending departments that you need to get in touch with, have an appointment with those people. If you just walk into your everyday branch those people are not qualified to handle a business loan. They might be able to handle your home equity for you, but on the business end you want to make sure you're talking to someone that truly can present your deal. The odds of you meeting with someone that's going to actually approve your deal are very slim. Most banks have centralized lending departments and that's who approves deals.

So again more important I always say, when I was a banker I always said, "You sell me, I sell you" because people had to sell me on their idea and then I had to turn around and sell a loan committee. I had to sell a department in Ohio, in some cases. I was working out of Pennsylvania and lending department was in Ohio. They obviously don't even know the market real well. So you're selling someone that you don't even see. So I always said, "Give me stuff so that I can sell you, make them see what it is that you're doing."

And with that information, I mean that brings up a really good question I think and what can someone do to prepare themselves for you, because it's like you said they have to sell you for you to sell them. So what can they do to prepare themselves properly to work with you?

Well whenever I meet with a client I have them bring me two years of tax returns, and I want every page so that I can go through and I basically teach them how to become a banker. They're looking; they're understanding how a banker analyses that tax return. I have a form that I provide them on any properties that they own, investment properties where they give me all the information, then I teach them how to do a debt service coverage ratio. So again I'm going to teach them how to, all the bankers babble that's out there. They have to go in educated. Whenever they're completed with our class, with the one-on-one because our classes are six hours one day, and then after that they get a one-on-one with me, and the one-on-one usually is one and a half to two hours. When they're done with that, we have a package ready to walk into any bank and then the components of that package really depend on what they want to do. It may involve some pictures of properties. It may involve historic data. I subscribe to an industry trend service. It may be information from that industry trend service. Every deal is different. So that's why it's so important after they're done with class format, the part of it is a one-on-one that they sit down with me, that we specialize that package to exactly what they look like, what their problems are, what their strengths are, and then how they need to present for what it is that they want to do.

Okay, and so definitely, I mean, it's not a fly-by-night-type operation these investors need to be running. They need to actually take, which I think is phenomenal, is that I think too many times investors come in and think it's an overnight process and what you're saying is, "look you need to take this serious."

Yeah, exactly.

You need to take, this is a business venture running, and if you want to run a very successful, profitable business you need to take it serious. So I think that's great and with that being said, you know once they go ahead and they get all their preparation and get everything over to you, why are they going to go ahead and utilize you? Why would someone prepare all that stuff and utilize you instead of finding a bank on their own?

Well the number one reason is credit score, because if they're going to all these different banks, very first thing that a bank does is run that credit. So when you're credit is hit your score is automatically going to drop just because there's an inquiry from the bank. Timing, if I do the package with them normally within a couple of days I know if I've got a bank approval. So if they're rushed in getting a property purchased they know right away whether to pass or sign on the dotted line. The package to the bank is now approvable, you know, many times they'll walk into a bank and say what do you need, and then they get a list and then they go back home and they start digging out things that they really don't quite understand. In my banking history I've had people, I've asked them for a tax return, and they give me a copy of the front page of the tax return. Well they just wasted their time and they wasted the banker's time because they brought the wrong information. So they aren't bankers. They don't understand what the banker needs. Some bankers can't communicate it real well. They're waiting for their next appointment, which may be the following week. So by the time they get that banker everything that they need to go for approval, maybe two or three weeks have passed. Where if I'm working with them, we get the package done, and off we go for approval. So I'd say turnaround time, credit score, approval versus denial. Those would be the three main reasons that they'd want to use me.

Okay, and so they prepare and they've decided to work with you and they're moving forward in the process, now one question that comes up a lot is what does a bank, how does a bank cash flow an investment property?

Okay, that is called the debt service coverage ratio. So they may see the banker say DSC debt service coverage.

A little different than DTI, huh?

Yes, and banks are ranging on their debt service coverage anywhere from 1.2 to 1.5, so another reason to know the bank you're dealing with and after I tell you how to do the ratio, you'll see that there could be a huge difference between a debt service coverage of a 1.2 and a 1.5. So how you calculate, you take your annual rental income, you subtract 10% of that annual rental income for vacancy which is little more than having that property not occupied for a month, so minus 10%. Then you subtract 5% of that annual rental for maintenance. Then you subtract 5% for reserve. Now banks have just added this really more recently because of the economy and it gives the bank a little bit of a cushion that if they do end up owning that property that the cash flow still substantiates, so again there's a cushion built in there, right now. Property management, if you're paying a property manager that has to be subtracted. Then property taxes, all of your property taxes on that rental property for the year; we need to subtract that number. Then we subtract your annual insurance, and then we subtract any utilities that the owner, the borrower, is going to pay. I see that many of the borrowers are paying for water and sewage. Some in certain cities are paying for garbage because garbage in some cities is a lien-able item and what that means is that if the garbage bill was not paid a lien can be filed against the property. So that of course would affect the owner, the landlord. So again to go over debt service coverage; annual rental minus 10% vacancy, minus 5% maintenance, minus 5% reserve, minus property management, if applicable, minus property taxes, minus insurance, minus utilities that you the landlord pay. Then that gives us a net rental income figure.

The next thing is how much are you going to borrow?

You've got to remember when you're financing an investment property that a bank is not going to give you a 30-year loan. You're going to get 20 if you're lucky, and most often you're going to get 15 years to pay the loan back. So to be safe, then you have to calculate your payment at 15 years. So we have our principal and interest payment, we have our net rental income. You then take your net rental income, divided by your principal and interest payment, and that ratio needs to be anywhere from 1.2 to 1.5.

So I just laid out a lot of banker babble, and you can see right there why it's important to have a one-on-one or attend a class or whatever you're going to do, because people have a terrible time understanding how to calculate this, but if you contact the bank and say, "hey my debt service coverage is 1.5" all of a sudden you're talking that language, you've perked their ears, they know you know what you're doing, you're a good manager, and that property is now attractive to them because you've got to remember all banks are looking at a deal as if they are going to own that property sometime in the future.

And that actually brings in a question and that is some great content actually, which I'm excited about. I definitely learned some stuff in there as well, which gets me to the question though is there a lot of different people right now that are so used to conventional financing and the terms and the terminology of conventional financing, and obviously getting the business loans from a business bank and you know you're going to deal with different terms, so what's the difference, some of the

major differences between conventional banking and what we're talking about here, business banking?

Well whenever you're financing an investment property and it is not owner occupied, then you have to normally go through the business banking system. Now when you say conventional banking normally that is just defined as going to your local bank or any bank. Then you have your secondary market where you can go through brokers, you can go through mortgage companies those types of things. So conventional banking you can find your business banker within those banks. It's just if the property is not owner occupied you're not going to get rates as low, because you now are into their business or commercial lending program. Every bank has their residential mortgage departments where I'm going to buy a house, I'm going to build a house, I'm going to live in it. People go there. Then they're going to have the office staffs, the consumer lending process where I need a home equity to buy furniture, I need a car loan, I need to educate my child, where you get your consumer lending type of products. Then they have a business banking division that does your commercial loans, so that would be loans for people that own businesses, that want to start businesses, that need business lines of credit to support accounts receivable or people that own investment properties. You've got to remember that is a business. Anytime you own a rental, even if it's just one, you now are a business owner. That is business income.

So normally you end up with that business banker, that every bank has a business component to it. Very, very few do not. I mean there are a few out there that may not do business loans. So there are many avenues you can take to find that business loan but again rates differ, terms differ, approvals differ. We just learned that debt service coverage differs. So you have to know the pros and cons of each area that you go. Some have a fee of 0.5%, others have fees of 10%. So it is just so important to know where it is you're going. Some are regulated. Some are not. So I had one gentleman that went for a loan and found out the night before closing he had a 10% fee on his loan, and it was because the place that he had gone through was not regulated. They did not have to disclose their fee. So he literally got a $100,000 loan and had to pay a $10,000 fee for that loan. So you really have to be cautious as to where you're going, what type of institution it is and again I can help guide in that.

And you mentioned earlier that they're looking for an individual who has a 700 credit score, now how is that relating in regards to have an individual credit score and actually if you're going for your business credit score?

Well honestly the credit score is the credit score. There are some banks that have a calculation for a business credit score. I do not run into that very often at all. In fact, in the Pennsylvania market we only have one bank that I'm aware of that is doing that right now. So normally it is your personal credit score that they are running. There are three different credit scoring companies, so if you subscribe to an agency that you get your credit score from as an individual those are the companies that the banks are going to use. The other thing you have to watch for is each bank has their favorites. Most banks just use one of the credit scoring companies, not all three and you can see as much as a 70 point difference between the different agencies. So a bank will lock onto the credit scoring company that they like and then that way they're comparing apples to apples. They're not using one credit score and company for you, a different one for me, and then they're seeing a mass of difference in how the scoring is done. They're going to stick to one.

So the credit score that I'm talking about is the individual credit score that do they pay their mortgage, do they pay their car loan that type of thing, and I can't greatly emphasize enough that people should know what their credit score is. They should watch their credit reports because mistakes are made, and in today's world of identity theft, you've got to be very, very cautious on what's happening to that credit report. Everything that we do, they run our credit. So you've got to stay on top of that score and then also in the world of technology, some banks just run that automated credit score, a human being does not even look at your application unless that magic number is achieved. So if your magic number is off by one point, you're a turn down. You didn't get a chance for someone to see that credit application at all. You just did not make their minimum credit score guideline. Now when I say that 700 is the minimum right now a year ago 650 was the minimum for some banks, 670 was the minimum for some banks, 680 was the highest that I saw and now you're seeing a lot of

700 minimums. If you deal with a smaller bank, then you do have human eyes that take a look at that credit bureau, but if you're dealing with a big national bank, as I said, that may just go through a system and kick you out and that's it the end of it. You just get a turned down letter and there's no dispute permitted.

And you that's just you're talking about the change on the credit side, so I imagine there are other changes that are happening inside your business now. How is that related what types of changes have you seen on your business side and lending related to investment properties?

Well I guess the economy has affected a lot of locations. So bankers are taking a harder look at where the property is located. They're having the appraisers are going out and they're looking at vacancy numbers. They're looking at how many properties are for sale. They always did that before, but now I'm seeing it affect the final appraisals probably a little more significantly. So appraisals are down slightly. Also bankers are looking at tenants, because with so many people losing their jobs, the tenants that you may bring in may lose their job. So you could have a very good tenant but if at all of a sudden they lose their source of income, they're not going to be able to pay their rent. So analyzing an investment property has gotten very difficult.

All of us if we own 10 investment properties and we owned our home, we're going to make our home mortgage payment so that our spouse and our kids have a place to live.

Then we're going to start making our investment property payments. So banks know that of course. So we're going to pay those things near and dear to our heart first and then as the money's available make those other payments. Losing or letting a bank foreclose on a rental property, you see a lot more of that happening than the foreclosure on a person's residence. That is going to be the last thing that they're going to want to let go is their residence. So again bankers know all of that. So the risk is there that the borrower is going to be more apt to let you foreclose on that rental property, you've got the risk of the tenant losing their job, and also we're seeing that it's taking a little longer to get that tenant to occupy that property. It wouldn't surprise me if vacancy percentages don't go up in the debt service coverage calculation.

You're seeing the risk of you know loss of salary, people relocating, people claiming bankruptcy, relocating. Communities if you're in an area with high crime, it may be a great street but all of a sudden it becomes a poor street. So there's just a lot more analysis going on and some banks have totally gotten out of investment properties. So it changes like the wind. You know what happened two months ago is different than what happened two weeks ago, and in fact yesterday I constantly interview banks, and yesterday I had a meeting with a bank and was going over their philosophy and they will not consider flips. As you know within the last couple of weeks they decided they weren't going to do flips. So again you need to understand those banks. Who's doing what, and obviously things change daily.

Yeah definitely and with that I mean that's why people would definitely come to you because, it's not their forte really to stay on top of that and this is something you delve into and been doing for 30 years, so it definitely makes sense for somebody to utilize you and let you handle that and, like I mentioned earlier, be a part of their team. So and here's another question that I get quite often from clients is: In regards to, what if they have, because right now you know Fannie and Freddie they have the four property limit, so what they ask is well what can I do, I want to roll those properties over into a commercial or business loan? Is this something that people are on the right track and have the ability to do?

They do. Now you've got a couple things you have to think about. Is if they have it financed, what they've basically have done is got their existing financing through the traditional mortgage method, so odds are that they own those properties as an individual. So in order to go on the business end, I have a lot of people that say, "look I want to take all of my properties and I want to transfer them into the name of my LLC, and want to refinance them under one blanket loan." Now you can do that but what a lot of people don't realize is that they're going to transfer from their personal name to their LLC, they're going to have to pay transfer taxes. Then I'll have people say, "Well that's okay. I'll just say I sold it to myself for a dollar." You can't do that you're transfer taxes are based on market value. So that's one thing if they're going to go from the traditional banking, financing and flip it over into a business loan package, and they're also going to change the ownership of the property, they're going to have a huge hit because of transfer taxes.

Now let's assume that the property is already in the LLC name or let's assume that they're just going to transfer it over, bundle them together and leave it in their individual name. That is no problem. A business loan you can have numerous pieces of collateral. I have one gentleman that owns 50 properties; on one of his loans I have six properties listed as my collateral. So we have one large loan dollar amount. We have six different mortgage filings against six different properties. He has one payment which obviously if you own 50 properties, you don't want to have 50 payments. So he has one payment that covers those six properties. Now everyone's thinking well what if he decides that he wants to sell a property or one of his tenants says, "you know what I want to buy this", under a business loan scenario you normally can go to that bank and say, "okay, how much do I need to pay down on my loan in order to have this piece of collateral, that one property, released." Banker will tell you what that dollar amount is; you can also get your payment dropped because you're paying down on that loan. So you can continue to have the blanket mortgage, now on five properties. So a lot of people are consolidating them, just really to help with their bookkeeping. It also helps with the cost of title insurance. It helps with closing costs. It's far cheaper to do one loan for six properties than six loans for six properties.

Yes it is.

So and here's another challenge that I know a lot of people are running up to, what they're doing is they're putting all their cash and they're pulling all their cash and they're buying a property in hopes to you know they're still in hopes to sell it really fast or something like that or get their cash back out or thinking they would refinance it. Now what do you recommend someone who has cash and wants to completely invest that into a property and anticipates being able to refinance that out, is that something they can do or is that something that is tough to do?

Well first of all let's address the flip. Right now flips are very hard to get financed, again economy. It's just houses are on the market as everyone knows now is the time to buy, and obviously if you want to make a big dollar on a flip now might not be the best time; although I do have clients that are doing real well at it. It's finding that bank that is willing to do the flip, is become more difficult. In fact I'm using a national bank and just to give you an idea, a national bank may charge four percent higher than going rates at your regular local bank, and their fee may be four times higher than your local bank. Now if the flip is attractive enough, that you can absorb that extra interest rate and those extra fees into your profit, and still feel confident then yeah, you can get that flip approved. So on flips they really have to be cautious. They have to find the bank that is interested and will do it and understand their guidelines before they go into that. As far as your rental properties, again you've got to know that there's a bank out there to support it. It has gotten tougher to get those approved, but again you've got to go in prepared. I always say that before they sign that sales agreement they've got to make sure that they've got a bank that's on their side and that's going to be able to help them out. So you know things are more difficult but there are still banks out there doing business.

Okay, yeah so it can be done but it's definitely got to be a good scenario on their side and more importantly for the bank.

Right.

Okay, now, you have a class and how in, I can imagine with all this information that's going into it, it's much better for someone to sit down with you and talk to you and maybe it might even take a couple of days for you to do that. So I know you have a class called How to Become Bankable, and what would that class, if we were to take maybe a two day class or a five day class with you, what's that going to teach me?

Well we have a one day class that's six hours on how to become bankable. In that class you're going to learn really a lot of the things that we talked about but in much greater detail. You're going to know how to put together your package for the bank. A lot of students when they're done with that six hour class then they have a follow-up one-on-one with me that is part of the cost of the class. So when they come to their one-on-one they normally have their package done. So in all honesty six hours of instruction is probably plenty for the average student in order to have that package ready for the bank and have themselves to the point that their bankable. The one-on-one, they bring me what they have completed, I review it, maybe make some comments, make some light slight changes, and then at that point I say to them, "okay, do you want me to find you a bank?" or "I know the perfect bank. Do you have a property?" So normally when the one-on-one happens we're ready to start financing. Some people are coming to the one-on-ones and they're bringing along a property, a sales agreement that they just signed on because they have learned enough in the class. Also they can call me on the telephone. A lot of people will call and say, "Hey can you go over the debt service coverage ratio with this?" Also on our web site, which is **www.businessbuilders.net**, we have payment calculations on there so if they want to see what their principal and interest payment would be, we have that there. We have different forms that they're going to need to put inside of that banker's packet. They can e-mail, ask questions. So we have debt service coverage, how to calculate that. So we have different things within the web site that they can use, the tools that they need to put together the package. So six hours in how to become bankable, normally is sufficient.

Now I have had a lot of students ask to have How to Become Bankable 2. How to Become Bankable 2, right now we are developing and in that we're going to utilize a real estate attorney to answer questions. We're going to utilize an appraiser, an insurance company. So we're going to have different professionals come in and they're going to answer some of the questions like explain mechanics liens to me, what document do I need to use so that I make sure that my contractor does not file a lien against my property. So that class is for your more advanced person that wants to make sure that they're covering all bases, not only did they buy the property but their understanding the title insurance, the appraisal end of it, and making sure that they don't get any unforeseen liens filed against their property.

Yeah and that's interesting. So you're taking the one class and taking it to the next step further for the people that are really doing things the right way.

Right and it's actually students, they're the ones that have told me what they would like to see. I have one gentleman that does a lot of rent-to-own properties, and they said, "Can we have him come in and talk to him?" The other gentleman that I told you owns 50 properties, and he's been in the business, I think six years, and in six years has himself up to the 50 properties, he always has a waiting list for his rentals. They want to talk to him and say, "okay what are your secrets?" So we're not only going to have the professionals but we're also going to have some local real estate investors that have it down to a science that are going to be available to talk to them.

And this actually brings me back now with once they have all that information, they go through you know one and two and they have all that info, how do they know

and how can they be comfortable in working with you to know that the bank will be interested in the deals they have?

Well I'm going to tell them up front if they're not bankable. I don't take weak deals to a bank because then I lose my credibility, and that's why so many banks that want to look at my deals is because they know I bring them quality. So if I have a student in class that has poor credit we're going to form a plan of action to get their credit where it needs to be before they start buying properties or I'll have students that don't have any cash. Well banks now are requesting that most people put in 20% into the deals. I mean it's probably nine months ago I could have financed a property for you based on appraised value alone. So if you made a good decision, got a good buy; say you bought an $80,000 property for $50,000 I would have been able to lend based on that $80,000 appraisal. In today's world, that's not happening. Banks are lending against that purchase price. Banks are more conservative. So you know cash is needed. So some people it may be that they need to consolidate to get some cash.

I just worked with a gentleman and we came up with refinancing his home in order to pull out cash. In fact he's going to have several steps. First step is we're refinancing the home to pay off the charge cards that he's been using to buy properties. So we're doing that consolidation. The second step is we're going to group together six of his properties, refinance them to pull out enough cash to pay off a business line of credit that he's been using to renovate properties.

The next step after that we're going to refinance some other properties. So the reason that we're doing it in steps is his cash flow is basically not there. He has borrowed so much from different sources that his tax return is not supporting the cash flow that the banker needs to see to approve his loan. So we got an approval on the mortgage refinance so we're like okay great, let's get you figured out personally first. So that is approved. He just e-mailed me the other night...he got his approval. As soon as that is closed then his cash flow is stronger. Then I can now start working on the business end of his business, his investment properties, take a chunk of those, get him some more cash out to pay off a $35,000 line of credit that is haunting him because it's an $800 a month payment which of course is affecting his cash flow, get that done. So step by step by step we're getting him to the point that now he can go out and start buying properties, and looking at them and signing sales agreements knowing he's going to be able to get financing. So sometimes it's a slow process, and sometimes you're immediately bankable. Everybody's situation is different.

Wow, what you guys do, it's amazing. So and that actually brings up a question I have. What all does My Business Builders do? Because you guys obviously are not a one-trick pony.

Right, well we offer training sessions for students. I guess first of all My Business Builders is to tell you the background. Obviously being in banking over 30 years, I've met a lot of people in 30 years, and Business Builders has been my dream for quite a few years, I love to teach. I did continuing education classes at a local community college for years. I teach at a university, a local university and I've always taught on things related to business. You know how to finance your business, gender differences in the workplace. With my experience in management I'm able to teach management supervision, sales, good salesperson... I've got all the sales techniques. So what I did was said, "Okay. What friends of mine that have developed through the years the same as me, and become strong professionals. Who's out there that would be interested in bettering the business community?" Because that's my whole idea, and today's world you've got a number of things. You've got people that are getting to the age they want to live their dream. It's like oh man, you know I'm 50 years old, I'm 45 years old, however old they are, always wanted to do this, you know I'm going to be in rocking chair wishing I would have done this and I didn't. So we're going to take people's dreams, turn them into reality.

Then we have the people that are in business and they're saying, "Oh man, I'm not making it. What am I going to do? I know how to make a widget but I sure as heck don't know how to manage my staff." So we can help those people and better managing the staff, then getting back to making some money. You know we have the people that are forced that they have to do something. They've lost their job. A lot of our students are your baby boomers. The baby boomers have had good jobs, high level incomes, and all of a sudden that job is gone and they're sitting there like I haven't kept myself educated. Maybe they're not real good at sales and the only jobs that are available are your sales jobs and then they have the generation X right behind them that is more educated and willing to take far less money in income. So the Xer's are getting the jobs that the boomers are out looking for now because they've lost that income. So the boomer in many cases needs to open a business. They need to take what they're strong at and turn that niche, that expertise into a business. But you just can't open a business without having all the components.

So basically what I did went out and identified the human resource rep that I valued the most from my years as a bank president, contacted her, and she's one of my consultants. She now is self-employed; so she's got the time to teach, consult whatever is needed. Then I contacted my favorite CPA. We actually were tellers together when we were in our teens and she now owns a successful CPA firm, and she is the accountant that trains in our classes. Then I have a gentleman that his background is in marketing and advertising. He has worked on some of the largest campaigns, national campaigns that are out there, raised a lot of money for nonprofits. He's a web designer. I brought him on board. Had another gentleman that has 40 years in the personality assessment industry and he actually had worked for a President at one point on personality assessments and such. So I have him on board and he provides personality assessments. We literally went to the point that we assess some of my top clients and we know what it takes to become a successful entrepreneur. Then the odd one is I added on a hypnotist. We teach sales and the hypnotist teaches the proper way of rapport building, so who better than someone into hypnotherapy, than to teach you how to gain rapport.

So we have this whole team of professionals that are available. They teach the classes. Our advertising gentleman has 18 years experience. We have HR with 25 years. We have accounting with 27 years. We have me with 33 years. We have the assessments with 40 years. So you have a group of professionals that want to give back and we formed My Business Builders and it can either be attending classes, which you get a very nice interactive workbook. We follow up with you. We keep on you, to make sure that you're working on your plan of action and we literally take you from the idea, the whole way to turnkey for the business or if you're an existing business owner from the very beginning until the end you're now stronger in management. You understand your financials, and all of this is followed up with one-on-ones from the consultants.

I was yesterday at one of my student's place of business for five hours with her and her CEO. We went over financials. We prepared a projection for 2009. We reviewed the different personalities of the employees. We identified who we want as supervisors. So you see there are all sorts of components of the program, and whatever a business is we just utilize that consultant a little stronger than the other.

Cool, so you know what's great about that too though, is people aren't just working with you they're getting all your team that you've built.

Correct.

You know, so I think that's unbelievable, that's great. And actually so I mean I think you pretty much you kind of got into it, you talked about you know everything that My Business Builders does, but you know I imagine with everything that you guys do you help out a wide-range of different businesses. So what types of businesses do you help?

Okay, well I can cover my last store with…I guess it's still a current class, some they're ready to go into class five in a couple of weeks here. This class had a realtor; it had one of the home jewelry companies, an engineering firm. We had a medical company, a retailer, an actual college student that has realized that she's a senior in college and when she graduates mostly like is not going to be able to find a job so she already is planning for what business she wants to go into. We have a designer, and we have a restaurant. So you can see any industry can profit from attending classes.

Our realtor is a startup, so he wants to start up doing things the about the right way. So he's forming his team so what he's focused on is okay how do I do projections. How do I hire the right people?

Our jewelry company is having difficulty with sales. So we're researching all of the different geographic areas that she is involved in. So we're looking at who is her market, who's her best client base and teaching her some sales skills.

The engineering firm just lost the gentleman that was in charge of their sales. So they're trying to, they have two people coming to see if they can take on sales themselves or whether they need to hire from the outside. In their whole process we're finding out it's a family owned business that our assessments are helping them to better work together, because nothing more challenging than a family owned business and deciding you're not going to talk to your mother because your two personalities conflict.

Our medical company was, the owner had passed away. The medical company was left to the spouse who knew nothing about it. She is having trouble with employees, having trouble creating credibility with the employees, needs to diversify some products, and also wants to change the business slightly so that it's her business now rather than her deceased husbands.

So you can see every student has something different and they're running off into different areas and then I've found out through the classes they started to network which is fabulous. It's like I know this person, I know this person so they're actually starting to increase their sales just by meeting the 12 people that are within that room. So that is very exciting, that sales are already increasing just by being in that classroom.

Yeah that's amazing and just, if someone wanted to come out or meet you what would be the best way for them to contact you, to take place in one of your bankable classes or all the other different opportunities that

you offer?

Okay, they could go to the web site **www.businessbuilders.net** and it'll directly e-mail into the company and then I would schedule one-on-one. I mean it could be on telephone. It can be in person, whichever they need and that would be the first step. Just e-mail me and let me know what you're looking at and give me a brief scenario and we get back to our students all of them within 48 hours. I'm out on the road a lot meeting with my clients, so during the day I may be on appointments. I give evening appointments. Our classes are on weekends to make it convenient. So, just e-mail and we will get back to you.

Okay, great and another thing I want to take a quick step back on a question that had just jogged into my head here is, you create packages, right?

Yeah.

So you're creating packages on the different, the person, the individual, the property everything so what, you have a partner that does some of this stuff, so what do you guys do in regards to creating that package marketing wise?

Oh marketing wise? Well on the marketing end we do web design. We in fact again back to my students, whenever you sign up for the five day class you either get a web site, you get your current web site update. You can have a new logo designed. You can have a new brochure designed. Our restaurant owner that is going through class decided they want a new menu. So as part of the class you get to work with our advertising person and develop whatever it is that you need. So again the restaurant decided to do a menu. Our medical company decided that they needed to have a better flyer for when they're out on their sales calls. Our jewelry company wants a better web site. They want to be able to take orders on the web site. So we're able to set up all of that for them.

So, on the marketing end he also was providing a one-on-one. His name is Derek and he provides a one-on-one to go over everything that you need in the marketing advertising. You discuss niches. You discuss diversification. He's a very bright young man that has a lot of creative ideas and for our restaurant owner he literally went to every restaurant that is a competitor of this restaurant, got menus, walked around the restaurants, saw what people were eating so that he can provide the data that this restaurant needs to know to improve their volume through their door. So again he customizes it to whatever that business needs.

Okay so you guys are really, really hands on which is great and on the real estate investor side, which I think is very, very important when people do contact you and on the bank side when they contact you, they need to understand that the extensive knowledge of what I think 33 years of experience that you guys have and I imagine you've got tons of contacts and I think what's important is that those people when they work with you are at their disposal. Right?

Yes, exactly.

And which is even better, you guys do the work for them.

Right, yeah but there's a lot when you take a look at all of the many years that the consultants have, we know people. I had one day that I was at a function and someone said to me, "Oh boy I need to have this information from the State" and I looked at them and I laughed and I said, "Well actually my girlfriend from high school runs that department." So there are advantages to being old.

Well with that comment I imagine here's one thing that I always wanted to know from successful people that I talk to, such as yourself, you know there's things that have led you, education I'm sure you have you're constantly investing in your own education, and you know what types or favorite books do you think that you've read that have really molded some of the ideas and concepts that you've come over and helped you succeed?

Well I have probably read oh sales books, I mean sales books are my favorites. I mean all the masters and with me having Dan as our hypnotist I am also getting into reading a lot of hypnotherapy books. Our sales process is innovative. It's not; it's nothing that people have seen. So I mean any sales book because I want to read everything that is out there. I love sales. My entire career has been sales, whether I was selling a commercial loan. I was selling a deposit account, or I was selling an employee to better perform at work. So we all were surrounded by sales. I can't say that one book is better than another. I love listening to motivational speakers such as Tony Robbins, but any sales book you can pick up is going to teach you something. I figure if I read a book and I learn one thing it's worth every penny that I've spent. So I read sales books. I read management books. I love reading books on gender differences. I also teach a class on gender differences, where I'm working with women and men on understanding the opposite sex, how to manage them, how to sell to them.

Derek actually teaches a class on selling to the generations and it's pretty darn amazing the difference between selling to a boomer, to a Gen X, and a Gen Y. So as far as a few books, impossible. Derek and I both have libraries, hundreds of books and his office is just a mass of books and so we read constantly, keep up on trends, keep up on industries.

Some of the things I'm reading are my industry trends. I subscribe to a service so I can stay up to speed on all the industries. So that I'm reading through the internet but it's a service that I have to subscribe for, and so I, if I have a restaurant owner I can pull the trends, those trends are updated every 90 days. So I guess there's no one specific, there's just a lot and you take it and based on my experience I know what works and what doesn't work, and so we created something pretty darn innovative in our sales processes by the amount of research that we've put into it.

Yeah, definitely and I can just by this little time we

spent together it's unbelievable the things that you guys are doing, and if you were to you know some words of wisdom per se or final notes for our readers, what would be some of the, you know, some of the first steps or final notes in regards that you would want to give them to as we round out here?

Be prepared. Remember the you sell me, I sell you banker philosophy. I mean I can't say be prepared enough. They cannot just walk through the doors and say I have an idea. One of the testimonials that I have on my web site talks about the number of banks that he went to and everyone laughed at him, they didn't even want to read his business plan. You know don't assume that just because you know you have an idea that someone's going to show interest. You've got to go in there. You've got to show them that you are bankable, and again be prepared. That's the two words right there.

You all heard it here first with Melanie Ansel, make sure that you're taking your life and your business, you know, well not life too serious because you have to have fun, but taking your business on the finance side serious because we're on a, you know, in these times and everything else, if you're trying to build the lifestyle that you want you need to make sure that your business is prepared and ready for that. So you know I definitely, Melanie want to thank you so much for being here today.

Oh thank you Nate.

Chapter Six
Interview with Darrell Hornbacher

This is Mark Evans DM here with a special Guest I'll tell you his name in a second.

I'm totally excited for you to be here!

Guys, truly what we are going to share with you today,

So they truly know, in today's economy where we're at everybody thinks we're in a recession.

It's funny I was having lunch yesterday and someone was talking about "well, you know how it is, we're in a recession." Now I live in a huge gated community, literally about 26 NFL football players in our complex and we're getting work done, the neighbor next door he just spent literally like $10,000 on decorations on the exterior that's only up for 30 days. My other neighbor spent $25,000 on his new mudroom for his house.

So I'm thinking, I'm hearing the people say "recession" but what my eyes are telling me is totally opposite.

And the only thing different that they know is they've figured out the game.

Folks, money is the game and that's what today we're going to be talking about is how to gain access and get up to $150,000 of not just like credit cards to Exxon Mobil or gas cards, but the real spendable cash to help you do more deals to make your life easier, to give you more confidence and such and we'll get to that shortly.

Please, turn your cell phones off, shut the door and we're going to have a total, I'm telling you brain emergence of how the rich get richer and how they're able to play this game to the fullest extent and gain access to huge, huge, huge, huge millions of dollars by leveraging something known as business credit.

So we'll talk about that. Again, grab a pen that works so you can make notes here in the book, and I will say grab your favorite Gatorade.

This chapter is going to be a wild ride. And I mean that. Before we get into this simply amazing way to get the cash I want to tell you how we got to this point.

I called Darrell via phone and we spoke about what he does and his credentials and I said we have to let the Real Estate World in on this ASAP.

So we went back and forth a couple times and now we are here.

So, guys I call him the "quarter billion dollar man" and you'll quickly see why.

I've never met him in person but we talked on the phone, through email and that's what's great about being a virtual investor is you don't have to meet people face to face all the time. And we'll talk about that later.

But today only, our main focus for you, and I truly do mean this, for you is to understand how you have access to money right now at your finger tips once you under-

Go Grab Your $247 of FREE Gifts at www.InsiderSecretsMoney.com

stand and realize how to get it. It's not hard; actually it's really easy! And you'll see today, but what I want to do without further ado, I want to introduce you guys to the "quarter billions dollar" man, Darrell. Hey Darrell, how you doing?

Hi Mark, thanks for having me!

Thank you for sharing what we're about to share. I know what we're going to share but I'm so excited!

Me too.

So, we're here. People are thinking, "what did I get myself into?" I'll tell them, I'll kind of go through here real quick before we talk about your story, is that ok?

Sure thing.

Ok guys, so today our goal is to do one thing only, learn how to generate up to $150,000 of spendable cash, FAST to use for any purpose of growing your real estate business.

I don't care if it's from buying more properties, rehabbing more properties, even to giving you enough money to get your business off the ground with marketing.

All by utilizing a simple automated "Midas touch business credit builder" that starts working for you instantly.

When I say "instantly" and when I say up to $150,000 cash fast, what does that mean to you? I have to be straight with you, you're not going to get $150,000 tomorrow and if anybody tells you, you can, run because they're fibbing.

But we're going to give you exact steps, actually it's 4 tears we're going to share with you of what business credit is and why you need to use them in conjunction as you're growing your real estate business. And what we're sharing with you, I've only talked with one other guy that kind of does what Darrell does today. And when I say "kind of" I say that very loosely. Darrell is a rare egg and you'll see why when we're talking here. So this is the "quarter billion dollar" man, Darrell. Darrell, can you share, enlighten us with who Darrell is, what you do, where you live and why you're doing what you're doing today.

Mark, I live in the great city of Denver, Colorado. I think its heaven on earth although I spend a lot of time in your neck of the woods also, although I enjoy it. I'm a mid western boy, grew up with solid family values.

Went to college, came out of college, got my first job with a fortune 100 company and was fired less than 3 months later. They didn't like my attitude so I went out and bought my first business when I was 23 1/2 years old and it was a dry cleaning store.

Made money, ran it for a year and sold it only because I was bored. And now 50 years old and in that time I've owned 13 different businesses buying and selling them all with the exception with one at a profit and one just crashed and burned. But along the way I learned a whole bunch on credit and about finance and about how small businesses can obtain capital. And I never found myself getting bored around money. So 4 1/2 years ago I started the Midas Financial Company and we do nothing but obtain capital for our clients. That's my story.

That's awesome, and not only that, you said something that's super powerful and we skimmed over it so I want to real quick rewind. You said you had a couple businesses that didn't sell for a profit, guys what he just said is so powerful and what I mean by this is, with business credit and understanding how it works, you can fail, obviously no one wants to fail on purpose, but you could fail and still see another day tomorrow and succeed huge! So it's about determination, it's about understanding how the game works and staying positive around people. So, I just had to say that real quick cause we've all failed, we've all failed, right?

Well, it's a great point Mark. The business that had crashed and burned and the main reason it crashed and burned is we didn't have access to capital. It was a distressed company, I went it, took it over, the books we're already just leveraged to the hills and they just wouldn't sustain any capital injection and it went South. And I got to tell you, of the 12 I made tons of money on I learned way more on the one that crashed and burned than the other dozen combined.

Oh, wow that's amazing, Darrell's talking about some

powerful stuff about attaining business credit, about attaining up to $150,000 in real cash plus a bunch of other credit lines and we'll talk about that today. So make sure you have a pen in hand and because we are ready to rock and roll.

You might be thinking well, I don't have good credit, I don't have cash in the bank, and I don't have all these things. The beautiful thing with what we're sharing today... you'll never get asked their social security number is that correct Darrell?

That's correct.

You don't care what their credit looks like, right?

I don't care at all.

Let me ask you a question, has anybody ever went bankrupt and started doing exactly what we're going to teach today?

Yes, dozens of people.

Dozens, right? What we're teaching is NOT new. This has been a tried and true system with thousands of people across the world. And he's done a quarter of a billion dollars. It's nothing new but what it is, is, it's kind of I don't want to call it a secret group, is that the right word? Kind of secretive, right? Not everyone talks about this.

Well, it's not really a secret, it's been around for a long time, and it's just now coming to the forefront. In days past if you had a 650 credit score and a pulse a bank was giving you half a million bucks no questions asked. Those days are gone. And when you have access to that kind of money, smaller amounts and things like business credit just aren't as popular. Now that all the banks have tightened up their lending criteria people are looking for alternative sources of capital, especially real estate investors. A year and a half ago I was giving those guys a half of a million bucks at a pop by signing their name. That does not happen anymore. All of a sudden their capital has dried up, they don't want to go out and get a real job. They want to keep doing what they're doing and this is an excellent alternative.

Absolutely, so what I know of for to be a fact, you will fail in this business if you don't have cash for capital. I guarantee it, without a shadow of a doubt. And when I say access money it doesn't mean that it has to be your own money. Like, when I say I do deals with no money down, that doesn't mean I'm not using any money. It's just not my money. It could be bank money; it could be other private money. So right now I'm telling you this is not being shared with anyone I know in our world today.

You're some of the first people to know well, you're definitely the first people to know this through me. Darrell, this is the first time we've talked about this together publicly, right?

Yes sir.

So I know this to be true. This stuff works, I've done

it and as Darrell said as well, there's less people doing this and more money available it just has to be done in a different format or formula. So let's get started, here's what's going on.

"Why the heck should I listen to Darrell today?" Darrell Hornbacher is the founder of the Midas Financial Company. He has secured over a quarter of a billion dollars on behalf of his clients in the last four years. Darrell authored the highly acclaimed "The Midas Guide to Credit and Business Funding." Darrell, can you tell us a little bit about that book like coming out with that to the market, it's not a cheap book either. People have money for that.

Its $149 bucks and we're actually selling it so I'm really excited about that! So, real simple Mark, you know one of the things that I spent a lot of time on in the past is properly preparing clients. And I find it amazing that they have such high intelligence and energy levels in their industry but are really quite mistaken on what it takes to get money and they think they can just walk into a bank and say "here I am, give me the money." Well, that doesn't happen like it used to so what I did is put this book together and thoroughly explain personal credit, business credit in laymen's terms, talks about every kind of capital available to a small business owner and then the final section of the book, I published the methodology, let's call it in exactly what you need in a loan package to go to a lender or a VC or an angel investor so when you walk in and you are giving them everything they need to make their decision. And actually I alienated a few people in writing this book and mostly loan brokers like myself, cause you know that's really what I am. But they were pretty upset that I put the formula out and allowed people to go directly to a lender themselves without using a middleman.

You know what's great about that honestly Darrell is you have an abundance mentality. We all know everybody wants money, right?

Yep.

Everybody wants more money, more access to more money, gives you more deals, which equals more profit. That's just the game. So when you use this, this is definitely going to alienate some people. But you have a purpose to what you are sharing today.

We're here to help you understand. So, if you found a deal for $50,000, there are deals everywhere for $50,000 I'll tell you where those are at too. But, they're EVERYWHERE. If you could buy it and know it was worth $100,000 how much would you pay for that money to be able to buy that deal today?

It's worth $100,000 of real value someone's going to sell it to you for $50,000 how much is the $50,000 worth to you?

Is it worth $5,000? $10,000? $20,000? $30,000? $40,000? Let me ask you a question, would you pay $90,000 and sell for $100,000 to make $10,000? Would you be ok with that?

Go Grab Your $247 of FREE Gifts at www.InsiderSecretsMoney.com

That's $40,000 out of your pocket but yet you have no money. If you don't have the money to close the deal then you don't have anything. If you borrow the money and get $90,000 and sell for $100,000 you still make $10,000. See I understand. It's called Shark. Just watch Shark Tank it's on TV. They're sharks, hard money lenders that world is depleting and changing drastically but access to money is so different plus, hard money is determined off of their personal credit score, right? I don't care what anybody says. Darrell, do you agree with that? The guy's say "let me see your credit score" they're going to ask to get the hard money right?

Yes, they want to know how you've historically how you've handled your finances in the past.

Ok, there we go.

So again, let me ask that question, if today the house was worth $100,000 and you had access to an option to be able to buy it for $50,000.

So let's say I'm a willing able buyer and say, "Hey my name is Mark, I'll pay you $100,000" you say "great, I have a house that's worth $50,000 and this guy wants to buy it from me for $100,000 but I don't have the $50,000 to buy it." What are your options?

Hard money guys are not an option anymore.

If your credit is not that good you better have an amazing deal and you'll pay up the nose for the money.

Not only that, you have to get appraisals. You're spending your hard earned money out for the hope or just the idea or thought to be able to get the money. What if you had instant access to be able to buy for $50,000 and sell for whatever you want?

So what that does is give you an opportunity to sell for a little less, still make way more and that's how you become valuable in your marketplace and keep doing more real estate deals. You're selling the same exact product for less money because you have less money involved in it because you understand your finances.

You understand where the money is coming from and how much you're paying. We'll talk about that here shortly.

Why Darrell, he's a quarter of a billion dollar guy in 4 years, He's a nationally recognized speaker on the subjects of personal and business credit and business finance. He has been interviewed by numerous industry leaders and provides educational seminars on credit finance.

A flow chart that will show you how all this is done. I'll tell you how to get that a little later but it will guide you and walk you through step by step on what you need to do to be able to position yourself to get the money. Again, it doesn't happen over night and it takes some time but there's different ways to do it. There's always different ways to skin a cat, right? So, here's what you're going to learn from today's webinar.

So Darrell tell us what you're going to reveal here:

Why in the world would a bank give you access to $150,000 with no personal credit? We're going to tell you why and explain why and show you why and all that good stuff.

You'll learn how to play the money game. You guys all heard of this one guy his first name starts with D and his last name starts with a T... Donald Trump! He understands it. He's never personally gone bankrupt but his companies have and he's still surviving and he's worth a couple billion now.

You get a simple step-by-step flow of how to get the cash fast!

Get trade credit plus up to the $150,000 in spendable cash! This is cash that you could use in your business.

How your business can grow without stressing if they have the cash! You understand how stressful business is without cash in it. Look around in any business you can tell businesses are about to fail because they're stressing about cash. They're discounting everything to bare bones minimal and they can't pay their bills because it's too low so they put themselves in a bad situation.

How to sell more real estate deals to prospects with this method. No one is doing this!

Never beg a banker or hard moneylender again to give you the money! Never put yourself in that position. They own you if you are in that situation

What an LLC is (a limited liability company) and how to use it correctly! I see so many people have them they don't know what they're doing. They just have them just to have them.

Here's what else you're going to learn:

How to have instant cash to close your deals with cash! Don't you think that puts you in a better position if you're writing offers to be able to pay cash and close immediately? You can get better prices; you can get more people to look at your deals. I just can't tell you how great it is.

How to have the banks begging you to do their secret deals! Guys, I have banks contacting me now with REO's and deals that are bulk listing saying, "Hey Mark, I want you to do the deal. I know you do deals and I know you close on them and I know you pay cash, so we don't have to go through all those hurdles." See, the banks would rather sell quickly and get their money than drag their feet to make an extra $100,000. Banks aren't in the real estate business; they're in the money business. So what if they gave you that money and you just reinvested that money in the deal. We'll talk about that. You break through the amateur clutter to get the top deals in your market there's a lot of amateurs in the real estate business.

Money is different now. It's no secret, it's different

but there are ways around it and that's what today is about and that's exactly why this book is so critical to your business.

How to obtain 4 trade lines to gain instant access to business networks. There are so many networks that the more credit they extend, the bigger their bottom line becomes you utilize it properly and used it to benefit you and them. Everybody wins.

Here's what others are saying about Darrell. Rick Raddatz a successful online business owner.

"I'm a small business owner, so my credit-report shows all kinds of goofy stuff going on". That makes it hard to get the right financing -- especially for million dollar home loans. The $1.2 million dollar dream-home that I had been eyeing FINALLY came on the market -- but it was the HEIGHT of the credit crisis!

(November 2008). When my pre-approved loan fell through 3 weeks before closing, I called 20 different community banks and brokers. I also called Darrell. And thank goodness I did! Darrell's connection got me a 30-year fixed loan at a great rate at a great time when everybody else said 'if only you came to us 3 months ago'. Thank you Darrell!!!

So what he's saying is when times are tough he came to Darrell and Darrell had a solution. There are solutions for money you just have to know where to get them and that's why you're here today so thank you. One more Darrell

Ok.

Anonymous NFL Linebacker:

"I sat next to Darrell on an airplane. In a 2-hour flight he had my financial/credit life straightened out. I can't begin to tell you how appreciative I was especially when I wanted to pay him and he wouldn't hear of it." People with millions of dollars still have financial problems. The only difference is their problems are different but they still have issues. Darrell has been my most trusted advisor in the area of credit and business financing for years. Whenever I need any help, he is the first person I turn to and for very good reason. He is simply the best and most honest resource there is."

Great stuff, so what we're trying to do is explain to you Darrell didn't just fall off the turn-up truck. He's been around, he's been in this game, we're in this game and you're here to learn how to get in the game. And that's what it's about and here's what it's not.

Darrell tell us what this is not. Then we will get into the meat and potatoes.

This isn't get the money and never pay it back. The $150,000 is to be used responsibly. Again, I have to stress this; this is REAL money that you have to be responsible with that when it comes into your funnel, you have to pay it back. You can't just go get it and go to Disneyland with $150,000. It's really being smart with your money. Giving you a fighting chance in your Business.

Darrell, we get asked this a lot, "Mark, I set this up and I get the money and I can't pay it back. What happens to me as a person?" Can you explain that real quickly?

Absolutely, nothing happens to you as a person Mark. Remember no personal guarantee was ever asked for and they never ask for your social security number other than an EIN and a business address. These lenders have no clue who you are. They know that you've demonstrated physical responsibility; these would be a good credit score. Do we counsel people who max it out and buy a Ferrari, absolutely not. We don't want you doing that and walking away. We want you to be productive members and procreating well and that's what this is all about.

Absolutely.

You'll make enough money in real estate that you can do those kinds of things. We're not advising get money and run. We're advising be responsible, be a productive citizen and I truly believe this 100% as well, we, you and I, real estate investors and entrepreneurs alike can totally change the real world recession that most people are feeling by providing value in the community, by buying properties, paying the taxes on empty homes, by selling properties to help make the market better, to get better comparables, to raise more values. It's a very vicious cycle in a good way.

Sorry Darrell got excited there for a second, proceed.

No problem, great stuff Mark. Get rich quick. We're all here, we know this is not a get rich quick. This is not a lottery ticket. This is real.

You don't have to use your personal credit. This is very, very important especially in today's economy people have no credit and if they do it's really bad. No more excuse of "my credits bad" I don't care, no one cares anymore. So you could use your business, develop your business, build your team and buy houses.

You don't need licenses. You don't need a real estate license, you don't need finance license to get the money. You don't need to be an experienced investor. They're not asking you, "have you done 25 deals?" "How long you been in the game?" None of that stuff it's irrelevant to getting the money.

All right, so here's the problem, you and I are real estate investors. You don't have to believe a word I say just drive in your neighborhood. Please do. You'll know this to be 100% true. The house on the left ran out of money. I know this guy. He ran out of money. He had a great paying job, he had financing in place, and he had a construction loan. He had it going, he was up and running, he lost his job. They re-evaluated his loan, cancelled his loan, lost his job, and cancelled his loan. This was his dream house. This was his dream house, he and his wife and his 2 kids and they do have a dog. They got it all built, ready to put the windows in and got their loan cancelled.

Go Grab Your $247 of FREE Gifts at www.InsiderSecretsMoney.com

You realize what that does to people?

Some people aren't as strong as each other but what I'm saying is people run out of money everyday. What stinks is if he understood what you are learning about today him and his family could be living in that home and be able to take complete his dream home.

We all have dreams, right? But it's what you do when you're dreaming. Are you just dreaming to dream or do you want to be responsible and strong and take the next step and say, "I can take it. I can understand it now. Let's do it!" I can't make that decision for you. That's you. But I can tell you this Darrell is the Game Changer that's what's great about this. Everyone has the same exact chance... EVERYBODY.

One more real life example there is a house in Atlanta with a for rent sign in the yard.

He's renting the house that is in worst shape then any other house on the block for more money then the others, because he's ran out of money and he's treading water.

Here's the numbers and why it's important to have access to cheap money.

This particular house is going for $1,200/month because that's what his mortgage is.

He'll never get $1,200/month as I own some properties in his neck of the woods on this property. I reached out to him and said if you fix it up you'll get more money and he said "I can't, I don't have anymore money." Well, the two houses I had down the street are not as nice as his house and we get $1,000/month per property.

But the game changer is we paid cash and we have no mortgage, no monthly mortgage payments. We have a little outlay every month like taxes, insurance, rehab, all the little stuff.

But we have access to cash to do the proper things to get it up to par and we could reduce the monthly rent if we had to and still be safe. You see, he bought it and maxed it out he has to pay $1,200/month if it's rented or not. We pay cash and with insurance and taxes it's about $300/month.

Who has more wiggle room, him or me? We're saying get the cash, use it wisely and you can get a portfolio of rentals, you can build a portfolio of houses.

This is the problem in real estate investing they have great deals just don't have the access to money, do you agree?

I agree 100% Darrell, by the way it's been 9 months and his house is still up for rent but he did reduce it. It was $1,200 and now its $1,149. It's not going to rent. Here's what's going to happen. I don't have a crystal ball but I can almost see it, he's going to lose it to foreclosure.

He's 2 months behind, the banks are calling him, he's running, scared, he's just frustrated. It's because he doesn't know the game and you guys do.

Once you start making more money you can build your business, build your empire, and build your portfolio. You build your cash influx. Cash is king and cash flow is king. Both are king. Having both come in multiple times and same time. It's a very good place to be in business.

So Darrell can you share with us the difference in personal credit and business credit?

Sure. Personal credit really isn't that hard to understand Mark but people just don't get it. There are small pieces to the personal credit pie, how long you've had your credit, the amount of new credit that you have and the types of credits that you've used. The two biggest once are your payment history and obviously you're going to have terrible credit if you don't pay your bills on time. But the one that people don't understand is the amount that you owe on your personal credit. Now for these purposes I don't really care what type of secured debt that you have; houses, cars, etc. What lenders really look at is your revolving debt; credit cards, department stores, things like that. There is a real simple formula; it's called the credit utilization ration.

Credit utilization ratio. It's really easy to figure out. If you have been granted a visa card and it has an original available balance of $10,000 and you charged $2,500 on it your credit utilization ration is 25%. $2,500 and $10,000 is 25%. What lenders are looking for in this economy more and more is how high your credit utilization ration is.

The minute it gets above 30% a red flag goes half way up the mask. Let's say and your credit score is going to suffer a little bit, maybe 5 or 10 points. Remember if you have 5 of these visa cards, I think the average American has 4.8 cards in their purse or wallet, and you've used over 30% of that available balance your scores going to drop 5 points. But if you have 5 cards you need to take that 5 points times 5 cards.

So your 725 credit score could over night be 700. The minute that you get above 50% that flag goes 3/4 away up the pole for your score.

I've seen people who have never missed a payment and paid all their bills on time and their scores went down 75-100 points slowly because of their revolving credit utilization ratio is above 50%. The minute you get above 70% your scores are going to tank. They go down as much as 200 points that I've seen but the average is pretty much right around 150 points. Keep in mind, when you take your utilization ratio back below the various platos your score will go back up. But, it will prevent you from getting credit from additional credit cards, from banks that will prevent you from getting a car loan, or even if you want to purchase real estate if you have to get traditional financing that is such as a heloc or whatever.

So that's kind of the biggest reason why business owners and real estate investors right now can't get cash. We're entrepreneurs, we believe we have created the next best thing since sliced bread. And we're going to sell our soul to the financial devil to get that thing done. And what tends to happen is the classic entrepreneur or business owners that I talk to.

I give this speech at least once everyday and I'll sit there and I'll say, "What's your credit like?" "It's 620 but I've never missed a payment in my life." "How much do you owe on credit cards?" "Well, Darrell you know I kind of maxed out 7 different credit cards so I can get my business started. My business is now doing well. I want to expand but the bank won't give me anymore money." "Well, guess why Mr. and Mrs. business owner because your credit utilization ratio is off the charts and they're not going to settle you with more debt."

So, with all that being said Mark with personal credit it needs to be used really wisely but in this day of age if you have a choice of putting food on your table or having a 55% credit utilization ratio vs. a 30% what are you going to do?

You're going to put food on your table.

And that's just one more reason for what we're going to talk about in a few minutes is so important. Business credit doesn't get reported on your personal bureau credit. You can have business credit cards, you can have business lines of credit, and you can have equipment leases, whatever the credit physicality is. If it's in the business mean it doesn't report of your personal credit and you can max it out with no worries.

Exactly. I don't want to get ahead of us but in a nut-

shell, using your personal credit will destroy you and your dreams because they're going to get tapped out even if you are paying your bills, no matter what. And to be honest with you guys cause I'm super transparent, I personally don't even know my personal credit score cause I don't need to. I don't need to use my personal credit for anything at all. All my bills are in business stuff. Everything's done like that so I'm assuming I have a descent credit score but you don't need it once you understand the game. That's what's so funny. Everybody is always stressing about his or her credit, you don't need your personal credit.

Problems with most trying to get cash with there personal credit. You have to have great credit. You are personally responsible for repayment.

What happens if they don't pay Darrell? They'll lose all their assets.

The sheriff comes a' calling.

Absolutely guys. I've seen it happen to great, great business people. They just mess up once. You can get everything right but if you screw up just once and go under and everything is in your personal, you will lose.

I promise you. You can lose personal assets. It's hard to get the money without a very long and vigorous process. Meaning, we've all heard the joke, if you go get a personal loan on a house what do I have to do, give a blood test? Give urine samples? It's kind of a real joke especially now.

Go Grab Your $247 of FREE Gifts at www.InsiderSecretsMoney.com

Benefits of Business Credit:

Requires no personal guarantee. It doesn't go back to your personal credit. No one cares about it. Requires no social security number. Requires no extensive background check on you. Meaning if you have this piece set up right you're fine.

Get more money as a business than an individual. You guys understand that's different mindsets. If you're an individual and you're used to making $50,000/year the mindset is they can only spend "x" amount a month. If not, they're going to cap over. In a business, if you have a business plan, an idea, and you're going to make $2 million/year and you have a dream or a vision, shared properly they invest money on that dream.

You can have terrible personal credit and still do this. Use the money for whatever you want. When I say whatever you want, we're all responsible business people listening of real estate investors. So I mean be responsible with it.

You can have multiple business accounts equal more money, you can have more then one. I have clients that have done this as many as 10 times with 10 different companies that they've created. And that's one of the points I wanted to make here. This product is nondiscriminatory.

If you go into a bank today as a start-up guess what?

Don't waste your time. Not unless you've already got enough money to do it on your own. You're not going to get money, If you are in a challenged industry, own a restaurant, in real estate investing, things like that, you're NOT getting money. I don't care if your credit score is 810. You're NOT getting money period today. This program does NOT discriminate against bad credit start-ups or challenged industries.

Think about this, what he just said is very important. Imagine going to the bank and saying "Hey, I'm a real estate investor, brand new and I want to get money."

They're going to look at you like you're from Mars. That's one of the highest risks in their minds. They don't get it and instantly they say "no" in a nice way.

What is great about using business credit is you can protect your personal assets from harms way. If everything comes crashing down you can still live the same life.

The best thing is, Darrell they could just re-due it. They could just start over?

Yep, also there are so many other ways I'll just touch on a couple here.

You can use your new money for down payments to buy more properties. If you do have great credit and you want to keep expanding, that's fine. You can use your new money for rehabbing. You can use your new money for marketing. So many people forget that they have to keep marketing. It's not that they forget they just don't have enough capital to do it. You can use the new money for building your business. It's a real business, which means you have to have a printer a scanner, a fax machine, internet connections, etc.

You can use your new money for buying REO's. You can use your new money for closing short sales and selling for quick profits.

Do you realize how much money people charge for you to use their money for one day?

You've heard of transactional funding, right?

Transactional funding say you had a house for $100,000 and you used their money for one day they're going to get 1, 2, 3, 4, or 5 points for 24 hours. That's like $5,000 to use their money for 24 hours. You know what's bad, what's even worse is you have to keep using the Transactional money if you don't have your own.

You can use your new money for improving your existing properties to get a higher value or to demand a higher rent. You can use your new money for systems to grow your business. You can use your new money for wholesaling. Buy today, hold on for 90 days, you know sometimes you can buy and you can't flip for 90 days. That's fine; you have to capital, conserve and hold it's not an issue. There's also other ways around it but it's not an issue at all when you have the cash.

Heck Darrell, they could use their money for a car to get from point A to B to help their business. I'm not saying go buy a Ferrari but if you're doing the general contracting yourself and you're driving in a Chevette you might want to get a little truck so it's easier to get from point A to point B. It's more professional, it's

easier, gives you more confidence.

This is to name a few of the thousands and thousands of ways to use your newfound money. This isn't a dream anymore. This is real.

Mark I have a question. You are way too young to know what a Chevette is.

I'm definitely not too young to know what a Chevette is, my cousin had one.

Sorry, I had to throw that in.

It was always a funny joke like; "hey you want to see my vet?" And it was a Chevette.

That was my first car like 30 years ago.

That's funny. Chevettes are funny cars. So Let's get into the 4 tiers of getting your money fast.

Here we go, there are 4 tiers to gaining great business credit and $150,000 in spendable cash guarantee.

Darrell, can you guarantee what we are talking about.

Absolutely. So tier #1: Net-30 accounts.

What does that mean?

Before we get into talking about tier 1 let me talk about the structuring of your business. There is one requisite for having this product working successfully and that's the proper structuring of your business.

If you are a soul proprietor this will not work and our guarantee will become invalid.

You need to be an LLC, S Corp, C Corp, whatever but you need to be a formal entity. This demonstrates to our lenders and ventures that you are a serious business owner. With that being said, prior to go into the 4 tiers, we do a couple of things. We go in, there are 3 business credit bureaus just like there are 3 personal credit bureaus.

The 3 business ones are done in Brad Street with their infamous paid x score. Equifax and Experian both have business credit bureaus just like they have personal.

The first actual step of the program and where we spend a lot of time and make sure everything is properly structured is actually setting up a business credit profile, putting the proper things in there, your business identification, your business phone number, your EIN, etc.

There's a lot of people out there that try and do this themselves Mark, and they fail because they don't understand or fail to access all of the little intricate pieces that we developed with this program.

We've got this so streamlined we know exactly what the lenders are going to look for when the applications come in. And just one little thing is going to throw up a red flag and then they're going to throw the file out and we have to go start from scratch.

Again, the first part is we do all the credit bureau checks, we spend a specifically amount of time doing that and we register your company with credit bureaus. Now we can do the actual process.

Tier 1, which is what we call net-30 accounts, or trade line credit. These are companies, and I'll mention some names: Dell computers, Office Depot, Home Depot, Shell Oil.

We have over 200 of them in our stable that we use on a daily basis. These are companies. We don't deal with any mom-and-pop type stuff. Every vendor or lender that we work with on behalf of our clients is a fortune 500 company.

So we will go to, let's say, Shell Oil and Shell will grant a minimal amount of credit simply using your employee identification, your EIN. They ask for no personal guarantee, they ask for no social security number. We apply using your EIN and they're going to grant you anywhere from $150 to $2,000 of business credit.

That's what it is. It's just trade line credit we get on your behalf, four of these over a month in a half period. Then we ask you to go out and use them. And this is the critical part of this, you need to go out and use the credit. It needs to be a minimum of $50. You don't need to max the card out, although that wouldn't hurt you. What's critical Mark is you have to absolutely be able to pay this account off when the bill comes due.

But basically what needs to happen with these trade line accounts is you need to make a minimum of $50 purchase. When the bill comes due you need to pay it off. And what happens then is all of our accounts, all of our ventures and lenders that we use through this whole process report to all three-business credit bureaus. They will report on the first, second or third of each month. And we'll talk in a little bit how to fast track into the program and make the reporting happen a little quicker. But once you've done that you have developed a basic business score.

Your Paydex score is going to be 75 to 80 with 80 being good. And your experience with Equifax business score and they're on a letter ranting, A, B, C, D, E and F with A being perfect is going to be on a high B or a low A. Once that's done now we can go into tier 2.

Tier 2 is revolving credit.

I know we talked about on the personal side. This is entirely different. So before you sit straight up in your chair listen to what I have to tell you. There are actual cash line lenders out there that will give you cash money with just your business credit score.

However, we've started low. We've got you a couple of trade line accounts, you've bought a tank of gas and paid it off, you bought a case of paper and you paid it off.

Okay, you're starting your history but that's all you're doing is starting your history. However, our tier 2 lenders, which are typically regional banks, they will give you revolving lines of credit or, what we call, low end revolving lines of credit in the amount of $1,500 - $2,500. Now, as part of the program we are going to obtain 4 of these accounts for you. So all of a sudden you could have as much as $10,000 in credit and you're going to be tempted to go out and do something, if you do it's just going to side track the program and we're going to start over.

You need to do the same thing with these low end revolving lines as you did with the trade line accounts or the net thirty accounts, you need to go out, charge a couple hundred bucks on each one of them and when the bill comes due you need to be able to pay it in full. Now, I mean you could charge your cell phone bill, everybody I know has a $200 cell phone bill or you could pay your light bill.

I personally pay all my bills, with the exception of my 4 mortgages and my car payment; I pay every bill with my credit card. I think I got like 80 frequent flyer round trips right now. But I like the idea of airlines giving me free flights.

The moral of the story is you need to use these accounts to purchase or pay another debt but then when that accounts comes due you need to pay it off with its entirety. That's absolutely critical to the success of this program. Now once you've done that, and these 4 tier 2 accounts have reported to the credit bureau, the 3 business credit bureaus, the 3 we talked about, then you're going to pass solid A credit with Experian and Equifax and you're going to have at least an 80 paid x score which is then going to move us into tier 3.

Tier 3 is what we call mid range revolving. We will establish another 4 revolving accounts on your behalf. Sometimes we will just take the tier 2 accounts that we've already established and ask for credit increases but there are the possibility that you're going to receive 4 brand new accounts. Now, each one of these brand new accounts will have credit limits that will average anywhere from $2,500 to $7,000 with the average one we're getting right now around $3,500 to $5,000 for a start-up, $7,000 for a business that's a little bit seasonal.

Now we're starting to talk about some serious money.

Between the tier 2 and tier 3 accounts you can have as much as $30,000 to $40,000 real easily. Again, you're going to be tempted, please, you need to follow the program because the big money is just around the corner. Make a charge on each account for a couple hundred bucks and pay them off. You can go out and charge $10,000 if you want to or whatever the case may be. At this tier you can start carrying balances and it is not going to hinder the rest of the program but the purpose of successfully completing, you never want to put over 30% in these credit facilities. You need to make the payments. You need to make them on time. Once that's done, you're going to end up with A+ ratings at all 3 credit bureaus and you're going to end up with 85 Paydex score or there about which is equal to an A+ credit rating and life for you is now going to get good for you really quick. Here we are, we moved into tier 4, which is high end revolving.

Can I just stop you real quick?

We're talking about a lot of things from index scores, tiers, credit ratings and all that stuff. Don't get bogged down with it. This is basic information but it's not basic if it's brand new to you. I get that; it's not basic to me just so you know. I'm taking notes just like you. What happens is you realize how important it is to have a specialized person help you with this. It's so insanely important. It just takes one mess up you have to go back to square 1. Our objective is to give you the tools and guidance to show you and help you and assist you through the proper path. Okay I just want to be very clear there.

I want to add on to that Mark.

Okay.

People think I'm crazy. Anytime someone joins our program, of course I like to make money but this isn't all about money for me. That's why I give each of my client 2 hours of my consulting time so they can get one on one, eyeball to eyeball here in Denver or whatever city I happen to be in or via the telephone. I sit there and go through this program with people prior to them enrolling line by line so they thoroughly understand.

I think that's enormous value. I told you, I think when we first talked I think you're crazy for doing 2 hours. It's a lot of work.

Okay. So now we're in tier 4 here's where it gets fun. And during the final tier 4 cycle we're going to establish 5 tier 4 accounts. These accounts, every client will receive anywhere from $15,000 to $40,000 per account.

Our averages are running right around, $24,000 to $26,000.

Think about it, if you pay tier 2, tier 3 and tier 4 you've successfully completed this program and you've got $150,000 in cash.

Now that's A LOT of money.

Now, I want to explain how you get this cash very quick. There are variables, what I call "delivery vehicles" Mark. Again, people don't sit straight up in your chair and run to the other room when I tell you how this money is delivered because it is nothing more than a delivery vehicle.

The delivery vehicle is a business credit card or cards. You can go out and get a business credit card on your own today.

Go online, go to the business section and an application is going to pop up and it's going to ask you for an EIN which specifies it's business credit card but just below that it's going to ask you for your social security number. It's also going to ask you to sign electronically at the bottom stating that you understand that you are personally liable for any charges on this card that doesn't get paid.

Our business credit cards do not, I repeat does not under

any circumstances require a social security number or a signature on the application.

Remember I don't have your social security number. I've never asked you for it and you've never given it to me. Business credit cards are real and they work and they are the delivery vehicle of choice for the banks. They all come with check writing privileges and they come with the non-usurious instant rates.

The interest rates on these delivery vehicles will be anywhere from 0% for up to 15 months and then after that 7.99% to 12.99% or they will give you an option of signing up for 5.99% to 8.99%. A lifetime interest can never be raised. Think about that for a second. You're talking about unsecured money that you haven't personal guaranteed and it's costing you way less than a hard money lender would charge you and you don't pay the fees every time you have to go and get that hard money loan.

This is a line of credit. It is just like the traditional line of credit that you see at all the major fortune 100 banks. They just chose to use the business credit card as the delivery vehicle. The biggest reason is because of the streamline approach. They do not have to have a lot of involvement with a loan officer with sending you a statement, etc. etc. It makes sense for them. They make more money because they have less employee involvements. Computer does it all. With that being said, you finished tier 4.

You have a high-end master card, visa, discover, American express and a second master card. You get the credit card and you get a checkbook and you can go and write a check to do whatever you want. Let me talk about one real quick and then we'll move on Mark. One of the things that people have said to me is "If I want to spend $100,000 of that $150,000 I theoretically could have to go to 8 different accounts and pull various amounts from each account. That's a real hassle."

HELLO?? This is free money that you got without a personal guarantee and dag gonet... if somebody says to me "I'm going to sell you this house for $50,000 and you know you're going to sell it to somebody on the other side of town for $100,000 ten days later, is it worth taking 20 minutes of your time to write 8 different checks to get $50,000? Again it's all how you perceive it. Is this a traditional line of credit?

Absolutely not, they're gone. And they're going to be gone probably for a long time. This is a creative alternative that it legal and we have the endorsement from fortunes 500s, lenders and banks and they're passing this money out by the day.

We do almost all the work. Let me take a minute and say what that means. We go out and set up your entity (if you don't have one already). We set up your credit profile. We obtain all of this credit on your behalf. However, this is an interactive process. You have to participate and I'm telling you right now, it's going to take up anywhere from an hour to 2 hours a month to do this and here's why.

A.) You've got to go make some charges.

B.) You've got to pay for those charges. There are 2 scenarios in paying for these charges.

The first scenario is it's the 12th of November and you got a Shell Oil card in the mail today, you activate it and tomorrow you go out and charge $50 worth of gas cause that's what we need to have on there. You wait until the 25th of November, your bill comes in the mail, you snail mail it back and your payment gets recorded on the 5th of December. Remember, earlier I said that all of our ventures report on the 1st, 2nd or 3rd of each month. By doing the snail mail process, you're going to miss the December reporting cycle and your activity isn't going to get reported until the 1st of January.

Oh boy, not we're going to have to wait.

Where as in scenario 2: you get the card, you activate it, you charge $50, you wait 3 or 4 days till it records, you get online to the Shell Oil website, you set up a username and password and you pay your bill online.

Guess what?

You're going to get reported in the December cycle. You won't be waiting till January. You're saving 30 whole days. Now, if you do that thru tier 1 to tier 3 you could save as much as 90 days in the time that it takes you to get this $150,000.

That's the inner activity. That's what's going to take you some time. I'm going to hold your hand through this whole thing. And I'm going to be talking to you on the phone or sending you an email and I'm going to say,

"Hey Joe or Hey Sally, you need to go jump through hoops, go do this today. The quicker you do it, the quicker you're going to get your money."

It's called accountability to get you to the next step. The quicker you get the money, the quicker you make more money. It's all about that. If that scares you it could be way less than that but you have to do your part. We always set it up worse case scenario. Just do your part.

Darrell is there a way to help you and walk you through it and all that good stuff? Are you guys accredited by the Better Business Bureau.

Yes sir. That's a big accreditation.

What I like about you Darrell is that you are there to help your clients.

Because when you know it works, it works and people listen. And they work it and they get money.

What he talks about you can't lose. We don't over promise and under deliver. That's why he's going into it a little deeper than I personally understand. You know, that's why he takes 2 hours on the phone with you privately; talk about what you need to do, etc. and give you a fighting chance game plan to take the next step. Again,

you're getting trade lines, cash and credit so you might need that new computer.

Get one; pay it off and just do all these things that will really help you escalade your business. Darrell can you share more with the clients on how to get this rolling like ASAP?

Absolutely.

It's an interactive program! I don't know how many times we can say that, you have to do your part. There are short cuts to it that's why I'm here to help you.

We obtain the credit on your behalf; you MUST use it responsibly in order to achieve MAXIMUM RESULTS! Do you think that having access to $150,000 would totally allow you to take your business to the next step? It's totally over the top.

They're not giving money like they used to... EVER! But they'll give money to people that know how to play the game. It's in the banks best interest. We setup 4 "trade line" accounts in a 6-week period.

You use them and pay them off. This builds a "perfect" business credit profile. It's so important to build that profile.

With that "perfect" profile we obtain "cash" credit lines. Cash credit lines allow you to buy properties as you develop this. Again, use responsibly and pay off. We're talking cold, hard cash. Program culminates with additional "cash" credit line increases and high limit accounts. So, the longer you have it, the more they use, the more responsible they are.

What I like about this and you will is once you realize how easy this really is, you'll probably do multiple over time Darrell, right?

I have numerous clients, clients that have bought up to 10 of them and just kept forming LLC's and keep enrolling. My biggest client runs a hedge fund and I'm like,

"Gosh Craig, why would you do this when you deal with billions of dollars?" He's like,

"Darrell, if I can get $750,000 I can leverage that money in my own hedge fund and I'll double it every year. Why wouldn't I buy 100 of them?"

And the other thing to point out with this, once your through the program you've got such a solid business credit score. Leasing is a no-brainer and I'm talking about going out and leasing an office space if you need a formal office. You can go to the Regents. You don't have to put your personal name on the line because you've got a business credit score when they pull up the profile. Further, when these markets loosen up and it's going to be this time next year before the banks are giving money to real estate investors in the traditional way, in my opinion, having a business credit score is going to make a difference if they give you money. Finally with this, once you're through our program we don't want you having anymore than 4 trade line accounts so we can be successful doing for you what we need to do. But once you're through the program we have over 200 of these venders in our stable that you can go out and get 20 or 30 of these and each one of them with an A+ score is going to give you anywhere from $2,000 to $20,000 in credit.

You talked about the rehabbers earlier, how would you like to have $20,000 worth of credit at Home Depot? The moral of this story is it doesn't stop at $150,000 you can exponentially grow this thing in a year, year and a half - and I don't guarantee this and I don't preach it - I'm just saying that I don't walk away from you after the 2 hours is done. I'm always there for you through email or brief phone conversations.

You've talked about this, there are dozens and dozens of so-called programs out there that talk about and say, "Well we can't guarantee anything but we'll try our best." Most of the time they're saying they'll get you "x" amount of money, it's going to be trade credit, there's going to be personal guarantee.

It's going to be a whole different ball game. It's going to be like comparing a watermelon to an orange. I wouldn't hook you up with people like Darrell because I don't get most of it and I don't believe 99.9% of them. But after talking to him, going through it, and seeing whom he's associated with. We all know birds' together flock together.

With their program too, they are the only ones I know of that offer 100% money back guarantee on this, is that right Darrell?

To my knowledge we are the only ones. We do that simply because I don't want someone enrolling in my program with 100% confidence in me and the program and I want them to work the program with me. And if they are not a 100% it's not worth loosing my Better Business Bureau accreditation over a lousy couple hundred bucks.

Trust me, it cost a hundred times that to get it. So, if you don't like the program, we haven't done what we said we would do, I'm going to rebate your money and no harm no foul.

They're BBB credited. How much have you not made by not having access to the capital or cash? How much money have you lost? Truthfully you're looking at your life, how much? There are so many things that you can do properly when you have the capital or have access. We haven't even talked about confidence or time freedom. I'm telling you it's costing you more not having it around. If we said it cost $10,000 for this to get $150,000, who in their right mind would not say "here's $10,000 give me $150,000" Who in their right mind wouldn't say that's a no-brainer? Have constant access to cash. Ways better than hard money without a shadow of a doubt but you have to keep paying it over and over with those hard money companies.

Darrell, this is great stuff. If someone wanted to get more information about you and have you help them

then where should they go?

They can simply check out our website that has plenty of content for them and allows them to contact me directly. The site is **www.midas-financial.com**

I only want to provide the best available resource's I even know exist. That's my job as your friend and mentor.

So if you are interested in getting some money make sure to get over to Darrell's website at **www.midas-financial.com** and learn more about this simple and amazing process.

Darrell, I want to say thank you for sharing your time and energy with us and I'm excited to know the best money guy in the biz.

Thank You Mark and it was a pleasure I look forward to working with your readers.

Chapter Seven
Interview with Bob Norton

Let me go ahead and set the stage here first by saying that the purpose of this training is I want to set the record straight on transactional funding for everyone today. It's a way of funding for real estate investing and quick flip transactions. Right now, there's so many different ways that you can capitalize in the marketplace. You can take some type of funding or proof of funds to help you really capitalize on some of the best deals that are available to us today.

By the time we're done today, here's why I want to go ahead and set the objective of what we're going to have for you, what you can anticipate learning, and also what you can do to start implementing this type of funding within your business so you can start making some money.

By the end of it, you're going to ahead; you're going to have your mind wrapped around some important concepts that are increasingly more and more important to your real estate investing endeavors.

First, we're going to start with briefly covering the basics of transactional funding. Transactional Funding 101, that's what I'd like to call it. We're going to also talk about what it is, when do you need it, and how do you get it fast when you need it.

Definitely, with the deals that are available right now, you truly have to be able to act fast to make good money as a real estate investor. When you have access to money, you need to get it quick, and we're going to go through that process and how quick you can get it.

There's also a difference between a proof of funds letter. You have good proof of funds letters and you have bad proof of funds letters. You're going to be able to know the difference between the two today as we wade through the transactional funding process.

We're also going to go ahead and talk about how and where to get proof of funds on demand, so you can make fast offers when you need to.

One more important thing is one of the "gotchas" to watch out for with transactional lenders. There's more people coming in the transactional lending arena here for real estate investors, but you want to make sure, just like anything, is you build your team members properly. You always want to have the people who are doing things on the up and up, doing things that are really right for your business, that are going to help you build a great reputation on top of that.

We're going to talk about some of the pitfalls that most people are not talking about, and that you should absolutely avoid with this transactional funding, and when you're looking for the right lenders.

And then another thing here which is very, very important is characteristics. We will talk about some characteristics of trustworthy sources of transactional funding, including who we use and recommend. Because, as I mentioned earlier, you're building a real business here and you've got to have great people on your team to have a great business, that are trustworthy, honest people. That's very, very important.

And also, I want to talk about extremely crucial considerations most people don't talk about when using transactional funding for bank-owned REO deals. And as you know, we do a lot of bank-owned properties.

So this is the way that we're going to go through, to allow you, to make sure that you understand the processes of that so you can really implement the other teachings and things that we have for you.

And also, another very, very important thing is how to find an investor-friendly title company that can work with your transactional funding deals. So we're going to go ahead and show that piece to you, because not all title companies fully understand the process.

So I what I want to do is make sure that you can find an investor-friendly company. And there are so many other ways when you find that investor-friendly company that you can use your relationship together.

Before we move into this training, I'd like to introduce my strategic partner for this call, Bob Hi, Bob. How are you doing?

I'm doing pretty good.

All right. Awesome. What I'd like to do is go ahead and get jumping into this here. I'm glad you're with us.

And before we do jump into this actual training, I think it would be definitely helpful to just take a quick second and highlight a little bit of your background, and some of the impressive history you have as a real estate investor. You're very involved and do some amazing things, especially in the flipping arena. Can you go ahead and tell the people listening, get a quick grasp of who you are and why you're even worth listening to with us here today?

So in a nutshell, how are you and what's the Reader's Digest version of your story in the real estate arena?

Thanks, Nate. Almost exactly six years ago, I was one of those fortunate people who got the real estate bug. I was making about $30,000 a year at a corporate job. Got an ugly house under contract, a foreclosure REO, and promptly quit my job that next day after I closed on my ugly house. Life got a little bit interesting after that. In order to basically get by and pay rent and not go to the homeless shelter, I had to figure out a way how to make some money to float my month to month expenses.

I started bird-dogging REOs to other investors, which quickly led into wholesaling. And for about two to three years, I quickly started wholesaling properties, and ended up wholesaling about 200 REOs in a span of two to three years.

So I really got good at wholesaling and making some quick cash, and really worked the REOS.

Around 2006, I had a couple of people approach me and they were asking me how they could utilize their money a little bit better. So I acted as a partner with them, and I got into hard money business. We also mostly lent on REOs, but we did another couple hundred hard money loans over the course of two years there, until about 2008.

As the market evolved, my strategy evolved a little bit. I still wanted to flip, but I got into something real interesting, turnkey sales, where I'd buy a house, fix it up, put a renter in there, and then sell it to an out-of-state investor who just wanted to buy and hold and have a cash flow scenario.

I did really well with that for a year, and we were probably doing about 10 a month. Let me just tell you that that was an interesting time in my life, doing about 10 rehabs a month.

And then, man, I got a little burned out with that, and I recognized that there was a new opportunity to wholesale foreclosures to homeowners. I like to call them "clean REOs" or "whole-tailing."

I'm a really simple guy. I like to buy low, sell high. These were still foreclosures, I just happened to get a deal where I could maybe some **carpet and paint around and turn around and make a quick $30,000 or $40,000 selling to a homeowner and passing the deal along.**

So that's currently what I'm doing right now. Along with that, while my money guys that's a good way to call them. While we got out of the hard money business, they've been kind of bugging me, saying, "What else can we do to utilize our money?"

And that's where transactional funding hard money lending doesn't make very much sense right now, it's more risky. But there is a new opportunity to be a transactional funder.

Basically, right now at this moment, I've done about 500 transactions. I would say that 95 percent of those have all been REOs. I love REOs, I love everything about REOs. It gets me really excited, working with them.

And while I'm flipping REOs to homeowners, we're also doing the transactional funding and helping people fund their deals.

OK. Which is a huge opportunity really for real estate investors to do the types of deals you're doing. Like you said, six years ago, you were making $30, 0000 a year. I think it's important because a lot of people can relate to that. They've been in that position. I was in that position. I found the way with real estate investing to move forward with that. There's opportunity everywhere, and it's really just being able to leverage the right systems and people and put the right, especially, money piece to get some of the best and easiest deals.

What would you say makes you a little bit more unique or sets you apart as a real estate entrepreneur? Because we do have a lot of different people that are real estate entrepreneurs, and everyone's got a little different way

of how they do it. What do you think would separate you from the rest of the crowd, the rest of the pack?

That's a great question. One attribute that a lot of people could potentially see as a weakness is actually a strength of mine, and that is I probably have a fairly severe case of ADD. It can be both a curse and a blessing. I honestly think that being a real estate investor and having success, it's a challenge for most of us. We're trying to find our niche, but we always like to get into there're so many opportunities in real estate.

In a way, I don't take complete responsibility for ADD, but while that's been both a curse and a blessing, the one way I've been able to overcome that and turn it to my advantage is a hyper-focus. When I get set on doing something, I put all my attention and energy into that. And because of that, I can really generate some fast, immediate results that are pretty impressive.

Really, I feel very fortunate that I've been able to see results that come quickly when I hyper-focus.

The other thing that I feel very fortunate, and I've been able to hone this ability a little bit, is I've been able to recognize the trends of the market. I got out of hard money before most people got out of hard money, and we came out clean. We didn't get hurt like just about every hard money lender I know.

I recognized that sell and turnkey investors, out of state investors, was going to sour when they couldn't get financing, so I got out of that. As the market shifts, my strategy shifts.

One of the things that I consider one of my strengths is to really see where the market's going and adapt to that. So far, it's been able to be a great blessing for me.

You said something there that I think is important for everyone to really understand, and that is hyper-focus. With a hyper-focus, I think too many times people are trying to be everything to everybody, trying to do deals all over the place, as opposed to really staying focused on one avenue and perfecting like you've done, before you move on to the next one. So I hope everyone listening takes that out of this: focus, focus, focus. It's so important in your real estate investment business. And the reason that I'm gathering here with you, is that you are so successful and do so well, with all these other things besides your blessing of severe ADD. [laughs] And being able to look at the sweet spot.

Correct me if I'm wrong, but because of your hyper-focus, that's probably why direct success comes your way so much faster and bigger than the average person.

It is. And it's something where I really, like you; I encourage people to do that. I had an experience where I went down to Arizona a couple of weeks ago. And as most people know, Arizona is a real hot spot for REOs. In one week, I was able to train two people who spent basically a week with me, and we got five deals with an average profit margin of $20,000 to $30,000 a deal in that one week.

Go Grab Your $247 of FREE Gifts at www.InsiderSecretsMoney.com

And I could tell you that I woke up at 6:00 in the morning and that's all I did until 6:00 or 7:00 at night and that's all I did for four or five days straight. I let all the calls go to voicemail, never checked my email, had about 2000 emails in email box. But it just didn't matter. I kind of shut the button off and turned the other one on.

And now I've come back and really kind of go, man that was really cool. And that was because I did nothing else and was able to generate some quick and immediate results. As real estate investors, we all need a good kick in the butt and then spurt stuff up pretty quickly.

Definitely, definitely. That's great. Let's get into this here, Bob. I know everyone on here is very excited to learn the nuts and bolts of transactional funding, so let's get down to it with the training here. The first question, and probably the most important question for anyone who doesn't already know, what is transactional funding? What's the big deal? Why is there such a buzz about it? What purpose does it serve and why should people listening really care about it?

That's a great question. I will try to put this in a way that really makes sense and try to break this down for everybody. Transactional funding, just to give some background, for a very long time the banks were obviously very liberal in their lending procedures. And a lot of times so were the title companies. And so, as with that being the case, as a wholesaler, a lot of times I was able to put a transaction together where basically I could flip my deals.

And I could do this through one transaction. Let me give an example here. Let's say you have a seller, and it's the bank, and then I'm the investor. Then we have your buyer. So there're three people involved. And I'm going to designate this a lot of time we try to explain this to people we call them A, B, and C.

So the seller of the REO would be A, party A. I'm the investor and I'm party B. And then you have your buyer who you're to flip it to. They're the end buyer and they're party C. So you have A, B, and C.

For many of the deals I did, and for a lot of wholesalers and flippers, for a long time they were able to with the assistance and savvy-ness of a title company they were able to do an entire transaction without having to come to the table with their own cash.

In other words, they'd line up the buyer, the buyer would show up with their money, and the title company would use the end buyer's money to fund the acquisition of the first deal between you and the bank.

We like to refer to that as a "dry funding." That was something that wasn't very uncommon. There were some title companies that could do it, but most of the time it was very straightforward, and everybody won.

But a new problem started to arise, and that is title companies are very, very cautious now. Just like with the banks, how the pendulum they were too loose. Now they're too tight. And a lot of title companies, while this has never been illegal, a lot of title companies are just leery of using the end buyer's funds to do a transaction like this.

They get notification from the uppity ups at upper level management saying, "That is something that we are not comfortable doing. We will no longer do transactions like that."

With that being the case, there's kind of been a new problem that's happened. What do you do if you've got a great deal and you don't have the cash to close? And that's where transactional funding really comes into the picture and becomes a valuable tool.

Anybody who is flipping deals really needs quick access to cash. And I could tell you that even thought I was doing five or ten deals a month, I wasn't really in a mood to try to scramble all my money together and go to closing. It's the nature of us as investors.

So with that, really the need has arisen where we see a lot of transactional funders and a lot of people who have said, "Hey, we need to step into the picture. This is a business opportunity, and we need to help people fund their deal from A to B, and then turn right back around and usually the investor can sell the property to C."

So in essence, you need that money. You need that one hour or one day funding to really flip your deal. But you don't want to come to the table with a bunch of cash. And so that's where the market is kind of gone a little crazy with a lot of people saying, "Hey, I want to give some money to people and be a transactional funder, that's where the buzz is about is transactional funding."

And what we're going to do is, we're going to share with you some specific things that you'll look for in transactional funders. How you can trust them and how you can develop a long-term relationship with them.

I do have a personal recommendation for you, and it's a solution that I feel to meet all of the important criteria, and that I trust with my own transactional funding needs. Frankly, I think they beat the pants of off anything that I've seen out there up till now. We'll get to that in a minute.

I think that's a great, great understanding. I thought that I knew a lot about transactional funding and I just picked up some good key tips there too. As I mentioned early, staying focused, and you mentioned being focused, I think that definitely everyone needs to make sure that they're taking notes as well. Hopefully you did get that.

How does an investor know when they actually need transitional funding? What's the fastest way for them to determine that?

The first thing I want to do, I'm always a roots and fruits guy. And one of the things I want to do is address what sometimes I feel is a wrong belief. And the root is that you have to have money to make money. Just because you don't have money, doesn't mean that you can't do a deal. Obviously, if you don't have money, you're going to need transactional funding. But, that doesn't mean that you have to have a bunch of money in your piggy bank. Another example that's pretty straightforward is whenever you run into an opportunity where you need cash, you found your buyer and the title is company is saying, "Listen, we're more than happy to do a double closing, a wet closing, but we don't want to use your end buyer's money to fund the whole transaction."

So when you need that float for, say, 10 minutes or an hour, that's also where a high need for transactional funding comes in. A lot of times, I will tell you right now, that most of the time the biggest need in the market right now for transactional funding is short sellers, investors who do short selling.

You can by far and away use it as REOs, but as some of you probably know with short selling, if you do it all right and you line up the moon and the stars correctly, you can get a deal under contract, turn around and sell it, bring everyone together, without even having to put even earnest money deposit.

It takes a bit of creativity and it's not really my thing, but if you're doing a short sell, almost always you're going to need transactional funding, because you're going to have to fund that deal for a little bit.

Another thing that people really need to do a lot where they need transactional funding is to really just cover up the profits that you're making. What's real interesting is I got a call the other day from a guy who, he's making $400,000 to $500,000 profit on a deal. And because he did it on an option it was a commercial transaction he could have done it as an assignment fee on the settlement statement.

So the buyer sits down and they're saying, "Wow, I'm going to buy this storage unit for $1.5 million." And then they see right on there this little line item that says, "Assignment fee, $500,000 to Joe Schmo."

Well, let me tell you that in my experience and in his experience, that will be a deal killer. The first thing they want to do is negotiate down the profit you're making. A lot of people have a real psychological issue with you making a lot of money and they feel like you didn't do any work.

It's something in the past that I've always whenever my profits margins have been more than $15,000 doing a flip on an REO, I've always done a double close, just because I didn't want my end buyer to see how much money I was making. So there's another need for transactional funding.

And really, when you just need access to more money than you have on hand... Nate, about an hour ago, I got a call from a guy in Colorado, and he's flipping, he's going a deal up in I don't know if it's a short sell or bank owned property up in the mountains in Colorado. And he's a big time player. He's got access to a million bucks; I think it's basically his own money. I think he's a liquid millionaire. But this deal happened to be $1.7 million. And hence he could get a million but he couldn't get $1.7 million, so he was short $700,000.

So he called us. He just said, "Normally, I would never call you guys. Normally, I would never need to pay you guys for something like that, but in this case I just need an extra $700,000."

So those are really the primary needs and functions of when you're going to need transactional funding.

And there are also some different ranges. We're talking about some bigger deals, $1.5 million, $1.7 million. But, what are the types of transactions that someone could do? Does it have to be large amounts? Or can they do it with $25,000 or $50,000? My experiences in Atlanta, the deal that we do, are really under $50,000.

Absolutely. I gave away big numbers there, but it makes just as much sense to do a low end deal as it does to do a high end deal to use transactional funding. The biggest thing is not having to come to the table with your own funds. Let's be realistic. If you're a multimillionaire, you're not going to give us a call. No need to.

But, if you're out there and I would imagine that most of you are like me and you're always house rich and cash poor. It's just the nature of being a real estate investor. We see a great deal, we've got to buy it. So we always have got equity in all these different deals we're doing, and we're always trying to buy more deals. Unfortunately, sometimes that means our actual liquidity is quite low.

Whether its $20,000 or $50,000 or $500,000 transactional funding just makes sense if you need to use someone else's cash for a short window of time.

Definitely. It goes back to the whole thing of using other people's money to make money with. What are some types of deals specifically? I get this questions often, are there any limitations on the deals I can do with transactional funding? What are some specific types of deals that people that are listening can utilize transactional funding for?

It's pretty much anything where you're buying a property and then flipping it. It could be anything. We've gotten calls from people who are flipping land I can't believe they're still flipping land, but they're flipping land commercial deals, short sales, low end $30,000 or $40,000 REOs, for sale by owners. You name it. Really the acquisition method and what you're flipping really doesn't matter. It can by anything and everything. For us, we don't really care. It's just where you have a need, where there're three parties involved and you need those funds to do a double closing for a short window of time.

I would say the majority of them fall into most of us do residential. Any type of residential where you're flipping it, we're pretty much on board.

OK, so the sky's the limit.

Yeah.

I think that's really important for everyone to understand that. Your credit is not being looked, your income's not being looked at, this is a deal basis, really.

And you're not even so much looking at the profit that's in the deal, your major focus is knowing that there're buyers for those deals, right?

Yeah. And I will go back to that example that I had just this morning. He mentioned to me, he said, "You know. He is a big REO guy." And he said, "You know, this deal is not the type of deal I am going to do probably going forward. He goes, "I am hardly making any money." I think he might be making $30,000 after all the closing costs and everything on a $1.5 million deal, so I can almost guarantee that is probably a short sale. But he just said... And we don't care. We could care less if he is making $30,000 or $300,000. As long as we work it correctly with the title company, we don't care what the margins are, and that is not our business. Our job is to just provide that access to capital that you need for a brief period of time.

Definitely. Let's go ahead and take this process and line it out for everyone. For instance, if I am an investor, I have a hot deal on my hand. I want to act fast. I know if I don't act fast, I have the opportunity to... I know that if I don't act fast, I am not going to make the money. So what I want to know is, like, see that I am going to need transactional funding to handle my double closing. So what kinds of hoops am I going to have to jump through to make that happen? So I know... I am like, "All right. At this point, I got a great deal, so I know that I need transactional funding. What is going to happen? What does the process look like? What am I going to have to do to jump through those hoops to get the transactional

Go Grab Your $247 of FREE Gifts at www.InsiderSecretsMoney.com

funding?"

Well, that is a great question, and it is actually much more simplistic than people think. As far as steps that you have to do as an investor, you would need to contact us. And you will learn a little bit more about how that works through our website. And all the necessary information that we need to, basically, go through a transaction, you would put in the website on a funding request online application form. Once that happens, typically, we don't really need to know about your deal and the closing and all those types of things until about seven to 10 days before the closing is going to happen.

Now, I recognize sometimes that there is a shoulder window. But usually, if it is before that, there is really no need to contact us, because there is nothing to do. And then the next step is we are going to contact your title company, and we are going to discuss with them, basically, how to handle our money that is going to come in and how to disperse that, and then how to handle the money that is going to come in from your buyer.

And we cover some specific instructions and make sure that it is very clear bout how to disperse those funds and how that title company is going to bring this transaction together.

But other than that, there really aren't too many more steps that are involved. Once we get to the day of closing, everything gets scheduled. We will send out our money. The title company will get it. They will coordinate with you, the buyer, showing up at closing. In essence, as an investor, you will show up to two closings. You will show up to the closing where you are going to buy the property, which would be, typically, with the same title company. And then you will probably, if you have ever done this before, you will go eat lunch and come back in a half hour, and then you will attend the second closing, where the end deal happens and your buyers shows up.

So there are the two closings. The title company brings it together. And it is actually a very simple, simplistic transaction. We just make sure that we cover our risks and that the title company understands exactly what to do.

So what you are saying too is if you are... Correct me if I am wrong, but you guys really handle the whole money process then.

We do. We don't want you, as an investor, to really get in the way! [laughs]

[laughs] Well, you know, I think that is good, which is great, because you are doing what you are good at. Transactional funding companies are doing... They know what they are good at and they stick to it, as well as an investor. They can stick to their main focus, it comes back to that focus point, and focus on either marketing for that next deal or marketing for more buyers to bring into their systems so they can grow their business even bigger. So I think that is awesome that the process is handled properly so people aren't going in and they are not stressing out about worrying about everything. That

is a great, important... Such a very important piece for every successful business is having great team players. And having REO transactional funding is really having a great team player like that.

You know Bob, I tell you what. I know that when you are using transactional funding for your double closings, the title company that you choose... I mean, it definitely matters. I am getting that from you. I am understanding that it definitely matters. And what are some of the essential or the hallmark criteria of investor friendly? I think investor friendly is a key point for title company that also is suitable for transactional funding deals.

Well, the first thing I would say is you are dead on. Using the right title company is essential. And I will get into that in just a little bit, what some of the risks could be if we don't use the right one. But, if it is a title company we have never used before, we are going to do our own due diligence. We are going to interview them and do some background research on them to make sure that we are comfortable with them.

One of the key things that we are going to make sure that we look for is that they have a good reputation and that they really know what they are doing. There are certain title companies out there where they don't really think outside of the box. We all know what type of title companies those are. Typically, they are associated with a very plain, straightforward, transactional type of real estate company, say, ReMax or Century 21.

And so, a lot of times, those retail residential title companies, if you approach them with something like this, they are going to kind of go, "We have never done that before. We don't know if we can do that."

So it definitely needs to be a title company that understands and has done it before.

A couple of other things that we always look for that are kind of like our musts are they must have been in business for at least two years, they must have a good standing with one of the major underwriters in the US, and there is about four or five, and they must have errors and omissions insurance, where they will have a policy that covers at least the amount that is being funded. Those are our three musts. We are always going to look for those.

So, if you know that you found a great title company and they do all sorts of cool stuff, but they have only been in business for a year, we are going to come back and say, "You need to find another title company."

The biggest reason that we look for all those things is because of fraud. Let me tell you that it is not hard to become a title company. It is a lot easier than you think it is. And we have run into some very disreputable and shady investors who claim to be a title company. And they know how to make themselves look, and smell, and act like a title company and all the right things to say, but we have kind of found, in our experience, that there is some major fraud going on. And people say they are going to be a title company and they are really not.

And, of course, we all know whenever you have fraud, typically, whenever you had fraud in the past, you usually have to have a title company on board. So, that is what we are trying to do, because you can imagine that if a deal comes through and it is $150,000, and we wire it out, and someone is telling us something... And it may not even necessarily be an intention of you guys, but a title company could take that money and run and we will never get it back. One bad deal can kind of ruin, sometimes, up to a year's worth of profits. So those are just musts. And that is what our lawyer has instructed us to do, so that is why we do that.

Definitely, especially when you are dealing with the multimillion dollar deals, as well. I mean some people do make stupid decisions and try to go that route. But everyone here, I know, that is listening to this call is going to be running their business in the utmost and wants to be dealing with the right people and trustworthy people. So do you have any specific title companies that you use or recommend others using?

Well, obviously, we don't know every title company that's investor friendly throughout the US, even though we'll fund deals throughout the US. But we do have a helpful hint that we'd like to pass along that we've made, at the corporate level, a relationship with, and that's First American Title Company. The reason why we recommend them is because we kind of ran our business scenario past them. They said they understood that. Also, one of the other things we recognized is there's typically a First American Title Company branch in every decent size city throughout the US. So, because of that, we pass it along. Obviously, if you live in Santa Fe, New Mexico, I don't know anybody in Santa Fe, and you may have a First American Title Company there. Never talked to the Santa Fe branch, but I have talked to national reps at First American, and we could put you in touch with them.

But we've found that First American is pretty flexible most of the time. They're good in the middle. They work a lot of retail, but they also do a lot of stuff with investors. Just a good example: First American has the national account with Fannie Mae. So, not only do they do retail, but they also do bank-owned stuff. So we've found that they're kind of a good middle mix that we like to pass that along to people.

OK. Great. And yeah, we've used them in the past as well. And I know that they are a pretty large company, and there are a lot of different places that they do work in. We talked about the title companies. Now, I wanted to try to give everyone a heads up, an idea to talk a little bit about things that they need to keep a look out for, some of the pitfalls, some of the kind of gotchas that investors should be watching out for when they're flipping these deals with transactional funding.

Well, obviously, one of the major, major ones is to be careful about the title company that you're going to use. And we've already discussed that. Another thing that I want to mention here is that on REO deals, you want to make sure that you don't close both sides with the same title company.

Now, Nate, I know that you said that you do some REOs, but just to think about this for just a second. Let's say you're buying an REO through some REALTOR. And I'm sure you've experienced this lots of times. They make you use their title company. And typically, that title company's service is sub par at best, because the bank has negotiated and hammered them to death, and you get $8 an hour people running title and doing all sorts of stuff.

And so, because you're going to buy an REO and the bank is making you use their title company, that title company's allegiance is not to you but to the bank. So you may approach them, and we may approach them, and say, "Hey, you need to wait till the end buyer shows up, buyer C, before you'll fund the first part of the transaction." They're not going to do it. They're going to say, "Oh, that's great and all, but you hired me second. The bank hired me first. And as soon as money shows up, we're going to hit send and the green button, and it's going to get shipped on over to the bank."

So, just to let you know, with REOs, you can't use their title company. And without going into a lot of detail, what we do with REOs is we have another title company that we would work with, your title company, and we kind of coordinate the transactions with two title companies instead of one.

So, a couple of other issues that we have that you may want to look out for with transactional funders. Just a heads up.

First of all, be careful not to do the pay to play. There are a couple of transactional lenders out there who want you to pay upfront fees just to have access to their capital. There're several transactional funders who don't do that, and there's no need for you to have to pay upfront money just to get access to that.

Another thing is be careful not to pay too much for your funding. Typically, the market has kind of figured it out, and what most transactional funders are going to charge is between two to three points. That's plus a small transactional fee of $300 to $500, to do the whole deal.

So, for example, if you're doing a $100,000 deal, you need transactional funds for $100,000. The two points of that would be $2000, plus, say a $400 transactional fee. So your total cost would be $2400. There are some transactional funders that charge six or seven points, or, in this example, $6000 or $7000. So there's no need to pay that much.

Again, sometimes, with transactional funders, maybe it's not a pay to play, but they may say, "OK, you got a deal. And that 495 fee, we need you to pay that upfront." There's no need to do that.

And I only mention that because sometimes, if you're flipping a deal to a homeowner who's getting conventional financing, you never quite know till the check is cleared if that lender is not going to do something goofy at the last second. And we, personally, would hate to see someone put up 500 bucks and then, at the last second, have the lender for your buyer pull out, and then you're out of pocket $500. So be careful for that.

Another thing is paying too little for your funding. We always like to refer to this as Uncle Joey. Let's say you've got an uncle, and he's got a little HELOC, a home equity line, and you call him up and say, "Hey, Joey, I need 50,000 bucks. Can I give you $500 to borrow your money for a couple hours?" [laughs]

In my experience, I've heard stories about this. Uncle Joey says, "Oh, yeah, yeah. No problem. No problem." You get ready for the day of closing, and then Uncle Joey goes, "Oh! I forgot to tell you that I bought a boat yesterday on my HELOC. I didn't really have that money."

And I'm sure, Nate, that you've probably seen that a few times, and I know that you do a little bit with raising private money, that sometimes you'll get people that will say, "Oh, yeah, yeah. I've got a bunch of money to lend." And then, when you get down to it, "Oh! I forgot to tell you that it's on its way. I don't really have it sitting in my account right now."

So you get what you pay for. And just like with a contractor, we all know that there's really cheap contractors out there, but we also know that usually there's some problems associated with that. And so, you need to be a little careful not to pay too little because, typically, they're not very reliable when that happens.

Go Grab Your $247 of FREE Gifts at www.InsiderSecretsMoney.com

Just a couple of other little points. You don't want to use an inexperienced transactional lender. There's a real value that comes from having people that are experienced, reputable businesspeople who are running this operation.

I'll tell you that, in our case, I looked at this and said, "Boy, I want to make sure that there really doesn't have a lot of complications here," so I brought in a partner who's got 30 years of corporate, pretty complicated business experience in the banking industry. And he kind of looked at this and said, "I wouldn't feel comfortable with someone who's only done this a couple times." Not that they couldn't work, it's just sometimes you run into some above average things that you need to deal with, with the title company, and you want to obviously make sure that you've got someone who knows what they're doing on your side.

Another thing that you need to look out for is lenders that have too little capital. And it doesn't happen very often, but you'll get people who will be advertising. And it's not that hard, on the Internet, to make yourself look really big. But, behind the scenes, they might have a little home equity line of a couple hundred thousand dollars, and that's all they're using to fund these transactional deals and there is nothing wrong with that.

The only drawback comes if they are doing any kind of search engine optimization or marketing, sometimes you get two or three requests that all come in at the exact same time, and then what do you do?

He has to pick and choose. Of course, they are not going to want to let you know because they are going to feel embarrassed. I have had a couple people call me the day before and say, "My guy was all set and come to find out he got tapped out of his money and I don't know what to do. I am scrambling. I'm up the creek" and there is nothing worse than going to closing or getting ready to go to closing and finding out that the money is not going to show up. That can ruin your day.

I would say and highly recommend that you need to have at least one million dollars. As a transactional funder, you need to have at least one million dollars of liquid cash that you can put out there on the streets right away. Not that you always need a million to do that but I've found that most people who do not have a lot of money and give the impression that they do, they don't want to tell you that they only have $100,000. That's a little embarrassing for them.

Those are the things that you really want to look out for. And finally, just one last thing is your transactional fund should not be dependent on your credit, the LTV of the deal, your income verification, or personal documentation.

This is not a hard money loan. I want people to understand that. Anybody who says, "I want to run your credit or I need to see that you are making money" and this type of thing, if you ever run into that just simply say, "Thank you" and run away because there is no need for that.

Yes definitely. There are a couple points here that you made here that I want to point out. One, I have heard some people ask me; transactional funding I think is

too expensive. While I think it is really not. Paying two to three points, you're not really paying to two to three points. I think people need to shift their mindset. Yes, it's two or three points but it is money that you would never see or make without the opportunity of using transactional funding.

That is a great point.

You can't count your dollars before... just like people counting the money before it ever gets to the bank account.

One thing that I want to add there... One thing that I learned as a hard money lender is people really want to know up front how much a deal is going to cost. They want you to be transparent. I had a lot of success as a hard moneylender because of that. They want to know, they don't want to get to closing, there is nothing worse if you have ever used hard money before, getting to closing and getting jacked with another $3000 or $4000 in fees. It has happened to all of us. It has happened to me. And you feel like you're put in a corner and there is nothing you can do about it. And you never want to use them again. So I learned that if you are very transparent about exactly what is going to cost, as an investor when you go out there and say OK I am going to need transactional funding here. Build that in as a cost of doing business. And what I used to tell people with hard money and I recommend now is if it is going to cost you $2000, $3000, $4000 to get the funds and you want to make $20,000 then you need to negotiate a deal to where there is a $24,000 spread versus a $20,000 spread.

And go into the transaction and looking to get that extra cost of doing the deal paid by the seller. Heck, make the stupid bank pay for it instead of you. Definitely it is a cost of doing business, but having the access to the funds is what is really important to people when you're looking to go in and do those types of transactions.

Yes, and as an investor you need to look at the money you're making as opposed to the money you're not making. So you can't trip over pennies to make dollars.

Exactly.

Another question I know that I get a lot before we get into some of this other stuff is what happens if I have an offer and we come to closing and my buyer backs out, my end buyer backs out. What happens at that point?

Well, that's a great question. I will tell you that has happened before with funding transactions that we have encountered. We understand that most of the time and different transactional funding companies handle these in different ways, but I will tell you what we do. We understand that is going to happen, and no one is more disappointed and no one has more vested interest in making sure that this deal happens than you.

Sometimes those things just happen. Obviously, there are a few things that you can try to do to ensure to tighten that up. Sometimes it is out of your control. What we do if that is the case, first of all usually they just will not show up. Usually, they just need another day or two.

So what we will do is continue to communicate with the title company. If the title company comes back and says hey they probably need one more day, the lender of the buyer, to get everything gathered up. And we'll just say OK. We'll make sure that they understand to not release the funds for the A to B transaction, and we will just keep it there, kind of on hold with the title company. If a couple days go by, we are going to ask the title company to send the money back to us and you are not charged.

We don't really see a need and in my opinion it is not fair to charge you for something that was out of your control. Now, if you are jacking us around and just screwing with us and the title company is just screwing with us then we are going to get a little frustrated, but we view that as that is why we want to have you step up out of the way and that is why we interact directly with the title company. But, there is no fee to that. Sometimes crap happens and we roll with it and realize that you didn't do anything and it was not your fault and out of your control.

Definitely. OK. I think that is great for everyone to understand, is just be upfront, honest and move the deal forward and you guys will be somewhat flexible on that piece if need be. Another question here is... let's turn this around a little bit, let's look at it here because we have talked about what not to look for in a transactional company. Let's talk about what you do want to look for. What are some of the characteristics of a trustworthy

and reputable experienced the transactional lender?

Great question. The first thing is to try to make it as simple as possible. Obviously, you need information to go ahead and move forward but to try and make the process I guess you could call it an approval process, but basically saying yes that is something that works for us is quick and with as minimum information and criteria asked of you as possible. The second one is that you fund 100 percent of the transaction. You are going to pay a couple of points; there is no need for you to come out of pocket with your own cash.

Third is it funds your closing costs. Sometimes hard moneylenders will do that to you. Let's say you're buying the house for $100,000 and you get $3000 in prorated taxes. Well, they also found that. In essence, they fund everything. Fund everything except your earnest money deposit, which you obviously had to take care of several weeks earlier.

That the proof of funds, and I am sure that will generate another question with that, the funding request saying. "Hey, I have a request and I need to do this and I need to get access to a proof of funds showing that I can put my deal together," that those are easy to get to and that they are ideally online.

Another thing is that the transactional funder will fund in every state. There is nothing worse than finding out that you are the one state they won't do deals in. That the fees are fair and competitive and that you have someone running the show who understands real estate in general. That isn't just a lawyer who understands all the technicalities, but he kind of gets it, has had some real estate transactions under their belts because every situation might be a little bit unique. It's always nice to have some who says, "Oh, yeah, I've seen that before. I understand what's going on," and can move forward.

Those are really the things; the characteristics that you want to look for when you're looking for a transactional lender.

That makes total sense, that's great. A great explanation. That's perfect. Let's focus, as you mentioned, on the proof of funds letter. We talked about it throughout the call, just hinting at it. So why don't we tackle that.

There's a few important things I think everyone needs to understand about the proof of funds, but first, for anyone who may not really understand it, let's go ahead and give them a quick definition per se, of what a proof of funds letter is, and why does an investor need it.

I don't know exactly what you're sharing, but I know that a lot of guys in your network may do REOs. So that's like the first standard thing, it's something that we're all familiar with. "Hey, I want your proof of funds." Basically, it's a bank statement or something that pretty much says here's proof that I've got money to buy this deal from you, the bank. That's pretty much it. Banks want to know that you can fund the deal before they make the decision. That's one of the ways they screen out the wannabes from the real deals.

So, that's something that's almost always going to be necessary. But it could be several different things. It could be a letter on some professional looking letterhead. It could be a bank statement. I've seen a couple where the CPA says there's so much funds here holding at this account, or a Merrill Lynch letter that says there's approximately this much on file. Or a bank that says this person has this much access on their equity line.

It could be IRA account statement or anything that's similar to that, saying, "Hey, the money's here and is liquid and is accessible." Most often, it's going to be a letter on some professional or kind of legitimate looking letterhead.

A couple of things to remember though, about proof of funds. And this is what I've found in my experience, especially with transactional funding. You need to have it where you can get it quick. We're always out there wheeling and dealing and the last thing you want to do is call up somebody and their assistant, and say, "Can you please send me a proof of funds?"

First of all, that's always bad because that assistant is probably doing a million other things. So ideally, it would be something that's kind of like on demand, online, that you can just go online and generate one. It needs to look professional, and it needs to be contingent upon approval of a couple items.

I will tell you right now that the proof of funds that we do, we have been there is no way that we are going to give you a copy of our bank statement. That would be wonderful in your opinion, but the legalities that run into that are just something that does not make very much business sense.

We're trying to get you the very next best thing. If you can't have the filet mignon with all the goodies for $100 at Ruth's Chris, what's the next best thing? And that's what we try to do to provide that.

To really see the anatomy of a good proof of funds, Nate, what is the URL, could you go ahead and share with everyone what your URL is so they could go and click on the proof of funds tab.

Yeah, definitely. For everyone listening, we have a special site set up for you to get even more information outside of here today. And also to provide for proof of funds letters. It's InstantInvestorFunding.com, which is exactly what the transactional funding is, for you. So go ahead and go to InstantInvestorFunding.com and click on the proof of funds tab, and it'll give you anatomy and everything that goes into a proof of funds letter so you can get a visual and understanding of it.

Exactly. Exactly. And I know that you were thinking about a few different URLs there. You go out to that and you click on that, and a couple of things that I want to just mention about the on demand. Like I mentioned, we're not going to give out bank statements, but the letter is very well done. We kind of searched really across the country and tried to get feedback from several investors and other people including people who do this day in and day out. We went to heavy hitting investors and said, "Give us feedback about what you think about this proof of funds and will it fly with the bank."

So we've come up with something that we think is very adequate. We don't do general blank templates. In other words, if you just want something that says, "Jimmy's got a half a million bucks," we don't do that. It's going to be deal specific. It's going to say, "Jimmy has access to $152,000 for this house on this street," and an address in there. So we don't do general blank templates.

We also ask that you're going to find this a little difficult to not go up there and sling mud. We've had people contact us and say, "I want to make a thousand offers with this cool software that I got."

Don't get me wrong, I understand that when you're submitting offers for REOs that sometimes there're several properties out there that you want to make offers on. But this is not set up to where you can go out there and get one general thing to go out there and sling a bunch of offers.

The other thing is the proof of funds, the on demand, get it right then and there on the Internet, it's limited to a half a million dollars. Just like the guy who called me this morning, we will not allow you to go above and beyond that. That's for legal purposes. Lawyers have advised us of that.

If you have a deal and it's about a half a million dollars, just send us an email. We're going to want to know a little bit more details, and then we'll be able to get you a proof of funds that's more specific for your situation.

That's really a good summary of the proof of funds right there, and how it can really help you.

Perfect. And while we're on this topic, what I want everyone to understand is when you do go over to InstantInvestorFunding.com, when you get over there, this is a website that I set up for you specifically. I set this up as a strategic alliance with Bob and his operations team, where you guys would be able to get these proof of funds letters to be able to utilize transactional funding. And even over that, there's some great Q&A questions for you to check out and some other knowledge to help you with, outside of this call, to look at this website, to refer back to if you have some questions.

So Bob and I are able to provide you with the transactional funding, that frankly it beats the pants off most anything we've seen out there. And as you all know, I've talked about transactional funding for quite some time now. We've looked at multiple different companies and talked to different companies.

The reason that I chose to create with strategic alliance with Bob is because I feel he truly is a leader in the industry, in the transactional funding. He does come with a trustworthy, honest company, with what he does.

That's why I want you guys to you're going to benefit by using it. So I just wanted to make that clear and for

everyone to understand that, that is for you to leverage the alliance that Bob and I have and get into transactional funding and start making some money on some deals.

And right here, Bob could actually take a second and share how this works for everyone at InstantInvestorFunding.com?

Yeah. I'll just give you a couple of quick highlights. I appreciate everyone's patience, and hopefully they've found this very informational thus far. Basically, it's a portal for your transactional funding needs. Everything that you really need could be right there. You can pretty much go through this thing all the way through, and do it all online. Which obviously, is very nice for all of us.

The transactional funding requests are quick and are easy. You will see there on the website that it is a very straight forward, easy to use website.

A couple other quick highlights are the proofs of funds are on demand. So you can literally get your proof of funds right then and there.

We found there were problems with people getting emails, or faxes with proof of funds so you will literally be able to get them right there.

We have a monster of an operator behind us. With the six years and 500 transactions that I have done and then obviously, one of the main operators and my partner has 30 years of business experience.

We also have a full time assistant who does nothing but run the show here. So you may say, "Oh, that's it? You have one full-time assistant and another guy and you Bob?"

Let me tell you that we are pretty much at the capacity where we can handle a couple loans a day, if necessary. By no means do we have all the capacity necessary. We also have on the site, very extremely reasonable rates. There is a comment fee or a processing fee of $495 that is paid at closing after your deal funds.

Just to give a little breakdown for everyone of the fee schedule. If your deal is up to $100,000, so it might be $25,000, $75,000 or $100,000. There is a flat fee of $2000. Anything between $100,000 and $250,000, it is two points. So if you were to do a $200,000 deal, two points of that that would be $4000.

Anything between $250,000 and $500,000 is two and one half points, and anything between a half million dollars and one million dollars is three points. If it's over one million dollars just give us a call. That's more of a case by case basis. Obviously, it is going to be at least three points but everything after that is a little bit more negotiable.

Those fees like I mentioned before are out there. They don't very. I have found that we are as competitive as anybody. As a matter of fact, I think we are the cheapest.

We have found that no one else is going to be more reasonable on their rates than we are. As investors ourselves we are pretty proud to offer these competitive funding fees.

I know that I personally am going to be using my own transactional funding on a deal that I have coming up here in the next few weeks. And it's exciting.

I bought a deal and sold it for $30,000 more without having to do anything to a homeowner and we are lining everything up and I am going to pay a couple thousand dollars and I didn't have to come up with my own cash. It's something that I use myself.

I want to make sure that everyone understands this is not a hard money loan. It's not a rehab loan. It's not necessarily a floating loan. Meaning we get a lot of people that contact us and say, "Hey listen, I got a buyer but the bank is just jumping down my throat and I have to close in a week. The only way I could get such a great deal was to close in a week. And my buyer, they need a couple more weeks to get all of their financing together. Can you float me there for two weeks?"

We will not do that. That is our definition of a hard money loan. That's why we don't want your credit. We don't want to know how much money we will make. We don't care if he had difficult times. We don't care if you only make $10,000 a year. And you want to tell your boss at 711 goodbye. None of that matters to us. All we care about is that they come together on the same day. Just to clarify that for everyone.

I also want to make sure that...one thing that I've found is a lot of times people will contact us and say, "Man this transactional funding sounds awesome. Can you tell me how to...how do I negotiate with the bank and how much earnest money should I put up and what should I put in the purchase agreement."

Like I mentioned before about hyper focusing, we have a real clarity of purpose in what we do. That's to work with people who already have the deal under contract that they are going to buy, already have their buyer lined up and they need our money. Anything else, questions and how to information and real estate investing tips, we're not here to answer that.

Not that I don't think your questions are very valid and I'm sure that there is other blogs and through the Internet there are different ways that as a listener that you can gain access for clear strategies of what you can do to get a deal so that you can use transactional funding, but that's not what we do.

We found that we can spend all day answering a bunch of questions, and we never make any money. So we are in this to make money. That is our purpose. And we want to help people but that is just one of those things that we are not going to give you tips and strategies on exactly how to do real estate tips or investing approaches like that.

We will answer all your questions when you have the two deals brought together. We are more than happy to assist and help you figure out how to put that together.

Thank you. I first want to take a moment to thank you for really taking the time to outline exactly how people can leverage in their business. To wrap this up because everyone has really been with us, they have been with us for some time and I know they have some great notes and I want them to absorb it all in. What I would like to do is one quick question that I don't think we did cover that if we can get a quick answer on is when do I apply for the transactional funding? What point in the process do I go ahead and submit my request for funding?

I would say that probably a good rule of thumb is, as soon as you have both your deal with the seller and your deal with the buyer, as soon as you have those officially locked up that would be a great time to contact us. I understand that your deal maybe...there is not much for us to do on our end if it is still two or three weeks out. But, you don't have to sit and say, "Man I don't want to bother them. When should I wait?"

If you have both of those together because just think about this for a second. If you contact us and say, "Hey I have a deal and I am trying to flip it and I just want to let you guys know." We are going to say well why don't you officially get it flipped and find your buyer and then give us a call.

Again, just a rule of thumb, as soon as you officially have your purchase agreement executed with your buyer and your purchase agreement executed or your option with the seller and all your paperwork is buttoned up tight, and binding so to say, then that is a great time to contact us.

I will tell you this that we need at least two to three business days' heads up at the bare minimum. We would appreciate a week. I recognize that sometimes stuff happens at the last second. We don't work on Saturdays. We work nine to five. We do need at least I would say three business days.

"Oh, I am closing in 12 hours from now or tomorrow." That's not enough time for us to get everything lined up with the title company that we need to get lined up. But that usually hardly ever happens. You get a deal and you get everything executed, great time to give us a call. That's the time to do it as soon as you get all that paperwork fully legitimate.

Awesome. I definitely think that helps out. Everyone, thanks so much and Bob I would really like to thank you and for taking the time out to clarify this stuff so I just want to thank you again. You can get the funding and connect with Bob and me over at www.instantinvestorfunding.com so I look forward to helping you guys out, and I am sure that Bob does as well.

Excellent. Thank you.

All right.

Websites You Need to Know About

Every single one of the sites listed below are very informative and needed for you to grow your Business. If you want to achieve the level of success that everyone you just read about has then you need to drop everything your doing and go to these websites right now.

www.504experts.com

www.trustetc.com

www.governmentdealfunding.com

www.privatemoneybank.com

howtobecomebankable.com

www.instantinvestorfunding.com

www.midas-financial.com

www.instantinvestor.com

About The Author

Mark Evans DM

Mark has coached and influenced thousands of Real Estate Investors from all over the world.

Mark Evans DM understands that the world of the Internet is ever changing. With his ability to comprehend how BIG of an opportunity there is online, Mark Evans DM has been able to take all the guess work out of generating multiple streams of Revenue by utilizing basic but powerful techniques.

Mark truly believes that ANYONE with the desire to learn and the determination to implement can go on to make money with their Real Estate Websites, even if you never do a Real Estate Deal. As long as you use the Marketing funnel, you have a fighting chance at building a buyers list, a sellers list and a Real Estate Investor list systematically.

Mark Evans DM has made it his mission to be transparent with his clients and share with them the power of the Internet Lead Generation World. Not only can it grow your Real Estate Business but it can put you in the position to make more money per lead than you probably even realize is possible. Mark Evans DM is known to be "Computer Declined", which is what makes his success in the virtual business world so impressive. His very own line of educational products and personalized websites are amazing business tools for the average user. These sites and products are simple, but they're powerful and more importantly systematized to help you work less while making more.

We are here for you and we look forward to serving you. To get more information about Mark Evans DM you can visit his website at www.MarkEvansDM.com

About The Author

Nate Kennedy

Considered by many to be an innovator and master networker, Nate Kennedy is the founder of many highly recognized marketing and mentoring programs that help entrepreneurs improve their businesses by keeping them ahead of the market curve. He is a #1 Best Selling Author and has other creative books in the works!

Nate considers himself very fortunate to be able to help people take the steps they need to become successful entrepreneurs and live the life of their dreams. His goal is to create a place that brings entrepreneurs together to develop relationships and become more successful through networking with people that truly care about your success.

He honestly believes that anyone can be a ultra-successful entrepreneur if they follow very simple steps and those steps begin with having the right information and technology that is going to keep you light years beyond your competition. Nate is very excited to share this know-how with motivated, like-minded individuals.

We are here for you and we look forward to serving you. To get more information about Nate you can visit www.NateKennedy.com or www.InstantInvestor.com